A pocket book on
HERBS

Sarah Dyer

OCTOPUS

First published 1982 by
Octopus Books Limited
59 Grosvenor Street
London W1

© 1982 Octopus Books Limited

ISBN 0 7064 1609 0

Produced by Mandarin Publishers Ltd
22a Westlands Road, Quarry Bay, Hong Kong

CONTENTS

What are herbs?

To most of us herbs are what we find sold dried in jars and packets, or perhaps a small collection of parsley, chives, mint and thyme growing outside the kitchen door or on the windowsill. It is not always realized that there is an enormous number of plants that may successfully be home-grown and used not only in cooking but in many other ways as well.

For example, herbs provide scent, and many herbs grown for culinary use may also be ingredients in pot-pourris, herbal baths and beauty aids. Herbs both fresh and dried have also been used medicinally for centuries. Modern scientific knowledge has meant that many cures now come from laboratories, but these are often synthesized chemicals found in the plants originally used to treat a specific ailment. Drug companies still depend on plants to some extent. Menthol, for instance, used in preparations intended to soothe a sore throat or clear a blocked nose, is extracted from peppermint.

In recent years there has been a revival of interest in herbs. Their value in cooking is once again being recognized as people become aware that bulk processing of food and the addition of preservatives and other artificial agents is good neither for health nor for the palate. Herbs are also becoming acceptable again in medicine and cosmetics, as the possibility of dangerous side-effects from synthetic chemicals is seen more clearly than in the past.

The meaning of the word

A herb, or herbaceous plant, is defined as a non-woody plant that dies down to the ground after flowering, but in the context of this and other herbals the term is used more generally to mean any plant which in some way adds flavour or nutritional value to food, though it is not eaten on its own, as medical treatment, or as a scent or dye. Many herbs may be used for all these purposes, and information on which part of the plant to use is given in the A-Z guide. For ways of preparing herbs, refer to pages 20-30.

Verbascum thapsus, *or mullein, (illustration by Sowerby) was dried and dipped in tallow and used as a taper.*

A short history of herbs

Since earliest times humans have used wild herbs for food and medicine. Discovering which plants could safely be used must have involved much experiment, the results of which were no doubt sometimes fatal. In an attempt to explain the mystery of why herbs had such enormous benefits and dangers, people made them the subjects of myths and legends. Those who took a special interest in the healing qualities of plants and learned how to use them became powerful wizard-priests and medicine men and reinforced the belief in the magical properties of plants and their religious associations.

It is thought that the first written account of herbs dates back more than 5000 years to the Sumerians, and that the first Chinese herbal was written in about 2700 BC. An account dating from 2000 BC appeared in Babylon, describing medicinal uses for many herbs. The ancient Egyptians imported many of their herbs from Babylon and India, not only for use as medicines but for cosmetics, dyes, disinfectants, perfumes and food.

The ancient Greeks and Romans added much to this gradual accumulation of knowledge. The medical writings of Hippocrates (460-377 BC), 'the father of medicine', and Dioscorides, whose *De Materia Medica* listed the medicinal properties of more than 500 plants, set the pattern for western medicine. Galen, a century later, wrote many medical books.

As the Romans extended their empire over most of Europe, they took their herbs with them. With the establishment of the Christian church in Europe and the founding of the monasteries, the use of plants for medicinal and other purposes became widespread. Greek and Roman writings on medicine were preserved in the monasteries which thus became centres of medical knowledge. The herbs left by the Romans formed the basis of the 'physick' gardens which the monks cultivated to provide the raw materials for treating illness. At the same time, the practice of folk medicine continued in the towns and villages.

Little new was written about herbs until the 16th century. In 1597 John Gerard, apothecary to James I, published his *Herball*, which described plants from all over the world, including America. In 1652 Nicholas Culpeper, a physician, brought out a herbal in which he expounded various astrological theories and also the Doctrine of Signatures, first put forward by Paracelsus a century earlier. This stated that every plant had a signature, that is, its appearance defined its medical application as it resembled either the part of the body to be treated or the cause of the affliction. Both these and other herbals enjoyed enormous popularity. The 18th century saw the beginning of a slow decline in the use of medicinal herbs as knowledge of chemistry increased, and scientists learned how to isolate the substances found in plants, and later to synthesize them. The custom of growing herbs for use in the home also began to decline with the Industrial Revolution. Table condiments, flavourings in bottles and patent medicines increased in popularity, and plant remedies came to be considered old-fashioned and inferior to the bottled kinds. But the move towards 'chemical' medicine did not go unchallenged. Homeopathic medicine and other systems using herbal remedies continued to thrive and survive today. Though chemotherapy remains the orthodox way of treating many ailments, the old herbal remedies, so simple to prepare and lacking in side-effects, still have a place in the treatment of numerous disorders.

Knot gardens date from the 15th century and follow simple or complex geometric designs such as these.

Growing herbs

Herbs are among the easiest plants to grow, and may be accommodated in the smallest garden, in window boxes and tubs, and in pots indoors. Wherever they are grown, the aim should be to reproduce as far as possible the conditions in which they are found wild. Many herbs are native to warm, dry climates and these should be grown in quick-draining soils where they will receive as much sun as possible during the growing season. In general, as long as herbs are planted in a sheltered spot away from overhanging trees, in moderately fertile soil with good drainage, they should flourish.

If you do not have room for a bed or border solely for herbs, it is possible to grow them among other plants in either the vegetable or the flower garden. Many of them are pretty enough to be grown as ornamentals, and have the added advantage of a fragrance. Perennial herbs, which either die down in the winter and come up again every spring, or are of shrubby growth (in the case of sage, bay, lavender, rosemary and others), may form permanent features of a herb garden. Annuals, which live only a year, and biennials, which live two years, usually have to be sown annually for a continuous crop, although many of the hardier ones sow themselves easily so that their effect is perennial.

Planning a herb garden
Having selected the site, which should be such that all the herbs will be accessible, make a list of the herbs you wish to grow. Do not overestimate the number of plants you will need, especially on a small plot. One or two plants of each perennial are usually enough for kitchen use, and perhaps three or four of each annual and biennial. More plants will be required for drying than for use fresh.

Herb lawns
Chamomile, thyme and pennyroyal are all suitable for planting as a lawn or a path in the herb garden. Herb lawns form a thick mat of foliage once they are established. Cultivation of all herb lawns is the same as for chamomile, as described on page 41, except that thyme and pennyroyal should be planted 30cm (12in) apart.

A herb garden 3 x 4m (10 x 13ft) can contain fennel, rosemary, tarragon, angelica (back); sage, lemon balm, parsley (middle); savory, marjoram, chives and thyme.

An all-purpose herb garden
Each of the following herbs has at least two other uses apart from its culinary ones. Basil, Bay, Chives, Dill, Garlic, Marjoram, sweet, Mint (spearmint), Parsley, Rosemary, Sage, Savory, summer, Tarragon, Thyme, common.

These herbs are suggested for specialist herb beds.

Medicinal	Cosmetic	Culinary
Comfrey	Chamomile	Basil
Fennel	Dill	Bay
Garlic	Eyebright	Chervil
Lemon balm	Lavender	Chives
Marigold	Marigold	Fennel
Marshmallow	Rosemary	Garlic
Parsley	Sage	Marjoram, sweet
Peppermint	Salad burnet	Mint
Rosemary	Southernwood	Parsley
Sage	Yarrow	Rosemary
Thyme, common		Sage
		Tarragon
		Thyme

Making a herb garden

Whether you intend to grow herbs in the open ground or in containers, careful preparation of the soil will help to ensure strongly growing, healthy plants. The best soil, called loam, consists of sand, clay, chalk and humus (decayed organic matter) in proportions which enable it to retain the correct amount of moisture and which will provide all the nutrients plants need. A heavy clay soil becomes easily waterlogged, and may need the addition of sand, peat or fine gravel to enable water to drain away more easily. Even though most herbs do best on light, free-draining soils, if the soil is very dry it will benefit from an addition of organic matter in the form of compost or well-rotted manure, which will also improve its fertility.

First, remove perennial weeds from the soil, then dig over the site, incorporating any additional material as described above. Fork over the soil to break up large clods and level the surface, then tread over the plot to firm the soil. Finally, rake the bed so that the surface has a fine crumbly texture (tilth); this is particularly important for seed sowing.

Growing herbs from seed

Most herbs may be grown from seed, sown either in early autumn or spring, when the weather is reasonably warm and there is no danger of frost. (Perennial herbs take much longer than annuals and biennials to grow from seed to the stage when you can start using them, so you may prefer to obtain young plants which you can use almost immediately). To sow seed outdoors, either scatter the seed or sow it in rows (drills) as thinly as possible. Cover the seeds lightly with soil, and mark where you have sown them.

Seed may also be sown in early spring indoors, in pots or trays, for an earlier crop. It is best to use seed compost, available from garden centres and department stores, rather than garden soil, as this contains weed seeds which grow quickly and could smother the herbs, as well as possible disease organisms which would flourish under the warmer conditions indoors. Fill the trays or pots to within about 1cm (½in) of the rim, firm it down well and water it with a fine mist spray. Sow the seed thinly and evenly; very small seeds may be mixed with a little sand for more even sowing.

Cover the seeds lightly with a thin layer of soil. Cover each tray or pot with a sheet of glass and enough layers of newspaper to keep out light until the seeds germinate. Keep in a temperature of about 13°C (58°F). Most seeds take about 10-14 days to germinate. Exceptions are perennials (up to 4 weeks) and parsley (up to 8 weeks).

After germination, remove the paper and glass and bring the trays into the light (but not direct sunlight). Keep the soil damp by using a fine spray which will not disturb the seedlings.

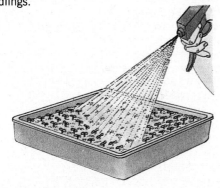

Transplanting seedlings

Whether they have been grown in containers indoors or in an outdoor seed bed, the seedlings will have to be transplanted to their correct planting distances to give them room to grow, after they reach the four-leaf stage. In the case of tray-sown seedlings, there must be a 'hardening-off' period before they are planted outside, to accustom them to the cooler conditions. Put the trays outside for a few hours each day when the weather is warm, increasing the period gradually so that after about three weeks the plants can be left out all night. They are then ready to transplant.

To transplant seedlings, carefully loosen the soil round their roots with a small hand fork, taking care not to damage the roots. Ease the plant away from the soil, holding it by its leaves which are less fragile than the stem or roots. With a pencil or dibber make a planting hole deep enough to take the roots without cramping them, put the seedling in, and draw the soil towards the stem so that it fills the hole. Firm the soil round the seedling with your fingers, and water well.

Planting pot-grown herbs

Buying young plants is more expensive than growing them from seed, but gives quicker results and is particularly recommended for shrubby perennials such as sage, bay and rosemary. It is possible to plant out container-grown herbs at any time of year, provided that the weather is not really wintry and the ground is not hard with frost. A warm, damp day is ideal. First water the herb thoroughly, then dig a hole about the same size as the pot, putting some leaf mould or compost into the bottom of it.

To remove the plant from its pot turn it upside down, holding the stem gently between the fingers. Tap the rim of the pot against a hard surface to loosen the soil ball, so that it can be removed with the roots in a single mass. Remove any drainage material and gently loosen the outside roots if they are tightly packed. Put the plant into the hole with the top of its soil ball just below ground level. Gradually fill the hole with soil, firming it down well. Water the plant.

Maintenance

Maintenance during the growing season simply involves weeding and making sure the soil does not dry out. Weed the soil round the plants by hand, and use the hoe for established plants only. To discourage weeds and to help prevent the soil drying out, a dressing of peat round the plants is helpful, as is a layer of black plastic sheeting which will also keep the soil warm. The leaves and flowers of herbs may be picked throughout the summer. Herbs which are required only for their leaves should have the flower-heads removed as soon as they appear, since flowering will cause the plant's flavour to deteriorate.

In autumn or early spring a thin layer of compost or fertilizer should be spread over the soil and lightly forked in. Many of the less hardy herbs, such as bay, tarragon and lemon verbena, should either be put in pots and brought indoors for the winter or given some shelter in the form of a layer of straw or leaves over the soil, kept in place with netting or thick plastic pegged into the soil. Some of the shrubby perennials will need pruning back to half the year's growth in autumn, to keep them compact and bushy.

13

Propagating herbs

Perennial plants may be renewed or increased vegetatively, that is, by cuttings, layering or root division. Well-established plants of clump-forming or shrubby habit are all suitable. Cuttings can be made of hard or soft wood, according to the type of plant.

Soft-wood stem cuttings may be taken throughout the growing season. Remove strong stems and trim them just below a leaf joint so that they are about 10cm (4in) long. Remove the lower leaves so that two pairs remain. Dip each cutting (take several, as they may not all root) first in water and then into rooting powder. Plant firmly into sharp sand or cutting compost. Keep moist and out of direct sunlight until the cuttings root.

Hard-wood cuttings are taken from woody shoots of the current year's growth, removed from the plant with a 'heel' of the old wood from the parent branch, obtained by pulling rather than cutting the shoot. They can be rooted in a sheltered spot out of doors.

Root division of clump-forming plants should be carried out in autumn or early spring when the plant is dormant. The plant is lifted and separated into smaller pieces, either by hand or by plunging two forks back to back into the plant and levering them apart. The centre of the plant is the oldest and may be discarded if growth is thin. Replant the divisions immediately in fresh ground. Firm them in well and water regularly until they are established.

Layering is suitable for plants with flexible branches which can be bent towards the ground. If the branch is thick, make a slanting cut on the underside of it, about 30cm (12in) from its tip, or twist the branch sharply at this point to break some of the fibres. Put hormone rooting powder on to the cut with a brush. Bend down the stem and bury it firmly in the soil, so that just the topmost leaves show above the ground.

Peg down the stem with an old-fashioned clothes peg or galvanized wire bent to a hairpin shape, and leave for several weeks until roots form. The stem may then be severed from the main plant and transplanted.

Another way of layering straggly plants such as sage or thyme is to cover the entire plant except the tips with soil. The bare growth under the soil will eventually form roots which can be used to make new plants, replacing the parent plant.

Herbs in mixed beds and borders

Herbs may be grown in a mixed flower border, either in groups among other flowers or as an edging. Some are also suitable for growing in rockeries; these include chives, thyme, winter savory and purslane. Woody-stemmed herbs such as lavender and hyssop may be used to make a hedge.

Herbs in containers

Space in a courtyard or other paved area may be put to good use by means of tubs and other containers full of herbs. Tubs, pots, old fireclay sinks, troughs, large strawberry pots with holes in the sides, window boxes and hanging baskets may all be used, provided they have drainage holes. Such containers are particularly good where space is limited or the soil is poor. Mint grown in a pot eliminates the problem of its spreading roots over-running neighbouring plants. The smaller containers may be moved around to give herbs the maximum sun or shade they require.

Use potting compost for container-grown herbs; mixing your own is cheaper than buying it ready-mixed, and is not difficult. Mix together 7 parts loam or sieved garden compost with 3 parts peat and 2 parts sharp sand, adding to each 36 litres (1 bushel) 100 g (4 oz) base fertilizer and 20g (¾oz) of ground chalk. Place large containers in position before filling them, putting them on bricks to allow good air circulation. Put drainage crocks (broken pieces of clay pots or stones) in the bottom of each pot to assist drainage before filling the container with soil up to within 2.5cm (1in) of the rim. Leave the soil to settle for a few days, then top it up if necessary, and water it well a day before planting the herbs. Make sure that herbs planted in the same container need similar growing conditions.

Container-grown plants need watering more regularly than plants in the open ground, and in the growing season the soil should never be allowed to dry out. Some of the plants will need watering every day in hot weather, particularly annuals — mints, chives and garlic. When water runs out of the bottom of the container the soil is sufficiently wet; simply moistening the soil surface is worse for the plants than no water at all. Feed container-grown plants every two weeks or so during the growing season with a liquid fertilizer, and keep the containers free of weeds.

Growing herbs indoors

Most herbs suitable for growing in containers will also grow well indoors, placed on a sunny window-sill but not in the direct glare of the sun. They will benefit from regular feeding and watering during the growing season. They will thrive if an even temperature of about 16°C (65°F) is maintained. They also need a fairly humid atmosphere which can be created by standing the pots in trays or saucers of moist gravel and by spraying regularly with water. In warm weather give the plants fresh air by putting them outside or opening the window, but avoid draughts. Repot indoor herbs in new soil every year.

Pests and diseases

There are few pests and diseases which attack herbs, and if the plants you buy are healthy and all seed sown is fresh, there are unlikely to be problems. The strongest plants are the most disease-resistant, so cultivate the soil carefully and feed the plants during the growing season with a liquid feed if you have not added organic matter to the soil.

Garden pests such as aphids (greenfly and blackfly) particularly affect nasturtium and valerian. They may be destroyed by spraying with a dilute quassia decoction or a soap solution, both of which are harmless to ladybirds, which prey on aphids.

Rust is a fungal disease affecting the mints, which become swollen and twisted and covered with orange spore pustules. The most effective treatment is to scatter straw or wood shavings among the plants in autumn and set fire to them, thus killing the spores in the soil and burning the affected shoots. The underground runners are affected neither by the disease nor by this treatment.

Parsley and lavender are prone to leaf spot, which is treated by cutting away and burning the affected parts of the plant and spraying the rest with Bordeaux mixture, obtainable from garden shops. Mildew, which may attack mint and tarragon in very damp weather where the plants are too close together, is also treated by spraying with Bordeaux mixture. Seedlings may be affected with damping-off disease, which makes them collapse at ground level. Discard the plants, and sow the seeds more thinly in soil that is not heavy or waterlogged.

17

Wild herbs and their uses

There are many wild herbs, considered to be weeds in gardens, that can be used as food and medicine. If you have no garden, or a weedless one, collect them from the countryside where you will find them in abundance in fields and waste places. Gather them away from dusty roadsides and land where weedkillers and insecticides have been used, in warm, dry sunny weather, preferably a few days after rain (so that any pesticides will have been washed off). Do not dig up the whole plant unless it is on your land; to do so is illegal. Take a few leaves from each plant rather than stripping a plant of all its leaves, which will kill it. Never use any plant that you cannot positively identify — it could be poisonous. The following are some of the most common wild herbs, all of which have several uses.

Chickweed *(Stellaria media)* is a vigorous annual found all year round. Its creeping, brittle stems are 10-30cm (4-12in) long and bear small oval leaves and tiny white flowers. It can be made into a decoction for constipation, a tea for flatulence, and a poultice or ointment for arthritic joints, bruises, burns and skin irritations. It may also be used in salads and cooked as a vegetable, like spinach.

Coltsfoot *(Tussilago farfara)* is a perennial whose creeping rootstock sends up downy, white, scaly flower stems 10-30cm (4-12in) high, topped by large yellow flowers which appear in mid-spring. The basal leaves are heart-shaped with toothed edges, smooth above and downy white underneath. Use an infusion of the leaves or flowers for coughs, colds, hoarseness, bronchitis and other respiratory problems. It can also be used for diarrhoea. The crushed leaves or a decoction can be applied to insect bites and stings, skin inflammations, ulcers, sores, and burns. The flowers can be used to make wine.

Dandelion *(Taraxacum officinale)* is a perennial growing from a taproot, with hollow stems up to 30cm (12in) high and oblong or spoon-shaped leaves, deeply divided halfway to the midrib. Each large, yellow, terminal flower is followed by the familiar puffball, a cluster of seeds each with a parachute-like tuft. All parts of the plant, which exude a milky juice, may be used, including the root. This is one of the most useful herbs, being entirely safe to use in large quantities. An infusion of the plant or the juice pressed from the leaves is an effective diuretic and excellent for treating liver complaints. It is also good for dyspepsia, constipation, fever, insomnia, rheumatism and stiff joints. It acts as a general tonic and stimulant, improving the digestion and appetite. Dried, roasted dandelion root is the best-known coffee substitute, and all parts may be used to make beer and wine. Young dandelion leaves are highly nutritious and may be used in salads and sandwiches. An infusion acts as a skin tonic and may be added to the bath water for a tonic bath.

Nettle *(Urtica dioica)*, or stinging nettle, is a perennial from 80-180cm (30-72in) high, with a square, bristly stem and serrated, heart-shaped, pointed leaves which are downy underneath. (The bristly hairs, when touched, inject an irritant substance into the skin, so handle this plant with

Six of the most common wild herbs (clockwise from top left) nettle, sorrel, dandelion, chickweed, coltsfoot and plantain.

care.) The small greenish flowers hang in axillary clusters from mid-summer to mid-autumn. The fresh juice or an infusion of the nettle plant is used to stimulate digestion and to promote milk flow in nursing mothers. It is of benefit in all kinds of internal bleeding, including haemorrhoids and excessive menstrual flow. It also reduces susceptibility to rheumatism and migraine, and the juice applied externally may be used for chilblains. Cosmetically, nettle juice may be·made into a face pack for oily skin, and the leaves used in a facial steam and tonic bath. The young shoots may be cooked as a vegetable or made into a soup. NB Old leaves uncooked can cause kidney damage.

Plantain *(Plantago* spp.) is a perennial with oblong, 7-veined leaves with thick, channelled stalks forming a basal rosette. The flower stalks are 10-45cm (4-18in) high with long slender, smooth spikes of yellowish-green flowers, from early summer to mid-autumn. An infusion of the leaves is useful for coughs, mucous congestion and diarrhoea. Externally a poultice of the fresh leaves may be applied to wounds, bruises, burns and bites. Use an infusion in an eye compress for conjunctivitis. Chewing on the rootstock will relieve toothache.

Sorrel *(Rumex acetosa)* is a perennial plant up to 90cm (36 in) high with light green, oblong, succulent leaves up to 10cm (4in) long and small greenish or reddish-brown flowers in summer. A root decoction is used as a diuretic, for diarrhoea, and for excessive menstruation. The leaves may be made into a poultice or infusion and used to treat skin problems such as acne. Use the leaves to make a sauce to go with fish and in a soup. NB Not to be used by those with rheumatism, arthritis, gout or kidney stones.

Preserving herbs

Harvesting Herbs have their strongest flavour just before they flower, which is when they should be harvested. Choose a warm, dry day and pick them as soon as the dew has evaporated but before the sun is really hot and starts to draw out the natural oils. Use sharp scissors to cut the stems, handling the leaves gently to avoid bruising them. Take no more than a third of the growth from perennials, bearing in mind that the cutting also acts as pruning.

Annual plants can be cut down almost to the ground, and will often give a second crop in the autumn.

Drying Hanging up small bunches of herbs is a suitable method of drying them, if a warm dry place with a good current of air can be provided such as a passageway or beside the stove. However, this is not recommended in the dusty, polluted air of cities unless each bunch is loosely wrapped in newspaper first, to keep out dust and dirt. This reduces air circulation round the herbs so that they take longer to dry and dry unevenly. A more efficient method is to dry them on a rack (such as a wire cake rack) covered with muslin (cheesecloth), laying the leaf stalks in a single layer and turning them daily to make sure they dry evenly. Keep them in a warm airy place such as an airing cupboard or the plate-warming drawer of an oven, with the door ajar. The drying time varies: when ready they should be completely dry and brittle but still green. They must be stored immediately, before they have time to reabsorb moisture or turn to powder. Strip the leaves from the stems and put them in airtight jars, preferably of dark-coloured glass. If they are stored in clear glass jars they must be kept in a dark cupboard; light causes the flavour to deteriorate rapidly. Do not crush or crumble the leaves until you want to use them, or they will lose flavour. Herbs for drying include bay, bergamot, garlic, horseradish, hyssop, lavender, lovage, rosemary, sage, savory, thyme, and all seeds.

Freezing All herbs freeze well, and the method is particularly suitable for those that lose their flavour when dried, such as basil, borage, chervil, chives, dill leaves, parsley, salad burnet and tarragon. Gather at harvesting time or whenever there is a surplus. Wash and dry the sprigs of herbs and immediately pack them into polythene bags, each holding a small quantity. Put the bags into polythene boxes to prevent them being crushed in the freezer. For freezing very small quantities, wrap them in foil folded to make a packet, and pack into a bag or box.

Salting An older method of preserving herbs is to cover them with salt. Use only the leaves of a plant and put them in layers in a wide-necked jar, with alternate layers of coarse salt between them. Pour olive oil over the layers and seal the container tightly. This keeps in the refrigerator for several weeks.

Medicinal herbs

Herbal remedies are of great value in the treatment of many ailments, for they are easy to make and apply and in the correct doses are remarkably efficient. Although all the herbs described in this book are harmless in reasonable amounts, it must be remembered that their efficiency lies in the fact that they contain active chemicals, many of which could produce symptoms of poisoning in enormous or prolonged doses. Specific side-effects of herbs and details of who should not use them are in the A-Z section.

Herbs which should not be taken for more than two or three weeks at a time are hop, horseradish, hyssop, rosemary, sage, valerian, watercress and woodruff. If any treatment makes you feel worse, then stop taking it. If symptoms persist or if you think your illness is more serious, consult your doctor.

Medicinal preparations

Many herbs can be used for more than one complaint; see the table overleaf then look up the one you intend to use in the A-Z section to find out how it should be prepared. For chronic conditions treatment may have to be continued for several weeks. Halve the dosage for children and the elderly. Always use non-metallic containers.

Infusion An infusion is made like tea, by pouring boiling water over the herb, which is then steeped for 10 minutes or more to extract the active ingredients, and strained. Where a treatment is referred to as a tea, drink it hot; when it is called an infusion it should be drunk luke-warm or cold. Honey may be added to improve the taste. The usual daily dosage is 3 tablespoons of fresh herb or 1 tablespoon of dried herb to 280ml (½ pint) of water, drunk regularly in small amounts throughout the day.

Decoction This is usually used to extract the ingredients from the hard parts of a plant: the roots, wood, bark and seeds. These are usually first crushed or, in the case of a root, scraped and chopped or grated before being put in water and brought to the boil in a covered pan. The herb is then boiled for about 10 minutes and then steeped for a further 10 minutes. To decoct green plant parts, boil for only 3 or 4 minutes and steep for 2 or 3 minutes. Leave to cool before straining off the liquid for use. Allow 25g (1oz) of the herb to 1 litre (1¾ pints) of cold water, and drink a small cupful three times a day before meals.

Cold extract This is simply soaking the herb in cold water for between 8 and 12 hours before straining. It preserves the most volatile ingredients more effectively than an infusion or decoction. Use about 2 tablespoons of the fresh plant to 280ml (½ pint) of water.

Juice Chop the fresh herb into small pieces, pulp with water in a blender, and press through a cloth to squeeze out the juice, which should be taken soon after pressing, and is usually diluted with milk or water.

Tincture The herb is steeped in alcohol instead of water, which means that it will keep indefinitely. Use about 40g (1½oz) of powdered herb to 580ml (1 pint) of rubbing alcohol or vodka, put in an airtight jar in a warm place and leave for 3 to 4 weeks, shaking it every day or so. Then strain and store. The dose is between 5 and 20 drops with water.

Syrup This is a useful way of giving medicines to children. Add 100g (4oz) of sugar to a warm infusion of herbs—about 280ml (½ pint)—and wait till it has melted before bringing to the boil and simmering until of a syrupy consistency.

Ointment Mix 50g (2oz) of crushed herb with 200g (8oz) of melted petroleum jelly, simmer for 20 minutes, and strain into a screwtop jar. Let it cool before covering it. Use externally for skin conditions and rheumatism.

Poultice Place crushed herbs on a piece of cloth, fold the cloth round them, and dip into boiling water for a few minutes. Squeeze out the excess water; apply immediately to the affected area. Moisten the cloth with more hot water as necessary.

Compress Soak a cloth or towel in a cold herbal infusion or decoction, wring out and apply to the affected area.

23

A table of conditions and herbs for their relief

	ANGELICA	ANISE	BASIL	BAY	BERGAMOT	BORAGE	CARAWAY	CHAMOMILE	CHICKWEED	COLTSFOOT	COMFREY	CORIANDER	DANDELION	DILL	ELDER	EYEBRIGHT	FENNEL	GARLIC	HOP
Acne, spots and boils									●						●				●
Anaemia	●								●		●		●						
Appetite, lack of	●	●					●			●		●	●	●				●	●
Arthritis								●			●								
Bruises								●			●								
Burns	●							●		●	●				●				
Chilblains	●									●					●			●	
Colds and catarrh					●		●			●	●				●				
Constipation			●						●				●				●		
Coughs	●	●				●				●	●				●		●	●	
Cuts and abrasions							●				●		●						
Dandruff						●													
Diarrhoea			●							●	●							●	
Eye inflammation					●		●				●		●			●	●		
Fever	●		●		●							●							
Flatulence	●	●	●	●			●	●	●				●		●		●	●	
Halitosis	●	●				●							●		●				
Headache (*for migraine)	●		*					*								●	*		*
Haemorrhoids						●													
Indigestion	●	●	●		●		●	●			●	●	●	●		●	●	●	●
Insect bites and stings			●		●					●	●			●		●			
Insomnia		●		●		●						●	●	●		●		●	
Nausea and vomiting		●	●		●		●	●							●			●	
Nervous conditions	●		●			●	●							●					●
Rheumatism					●						●	●	●		●				
Sore throat and mouth	●									●							●		
Toothache							●												●
Varicose veins																			
Warts													●					●	
Tonic herbs											●		●						

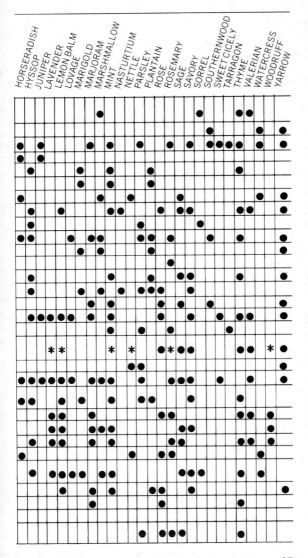

Herbs for beauty

Many cheap and effective beauty preparations can be made at home using fresh or dried herbs and other ingredients to be found in the kitchen. Since home-made cosmetics do not contain preservatives they do not keep as well. Herbs for oily skin include chamomile, elderflower, nettle, parsley, peppermint, rosemary, rose, sage and yarrow. Herbs for dry skin include borage, coltsfoot, comfrey, fennel, marigold, marshmallow and salad burnet.

Basic skin cleansing lotion For oily skin, add 3 tablespoons of chopped fresh herb to 280ml (½ pint) of milk, warm over a gentle heat until you can smell the herb strongly (do not allow to boil), then cool and strain into a screwtop bottle. Keeps for up to a week if refrigerated.
For dry and normal skin, to 25g (1oz) each of lanolin and cocoa butter, add 4 tablespoons of sweet almond oil. Put in a bowl over a pan of boiling water and leave to melt. Cool slightly and add 4 tablespoons of a strong herbal infusion. Blend thoroughly and store in a screwtop jar. Shake before use.

Toner Use a strong herbal infusion as a skin toning lotion.

Facial steam Not suitable for dry or sensitive skin, a facial steam once or twice a week unblocks the pores and helps to remove accumulated dirt. It also stimulates the circulation and softens the skin. Make an infusion of herbs in a large bowl and, covering your head with a towel, allow the vapour to soak your face for about 10 minutes. Pat the skin dry and apply an astringent lotion to close the pores.

Moisturizer Mix 1 teaspoon of honey or 1 tablespoon of lanolin or glycerine with 2 tablespoons of a strong herb infusion, or rosewater.

Face packs These should be left on the skin for about 15 minutes and rinsed off with water before moisturizer is applied. If you have dry skin, smooth a thin film of oil over the skin first. To make a face pack, a strong infusion of suitable herbs is mixed with a spreading agent. Those for oily skin are: a thick paste of oatmeal or almond meal and milk; beaten egg white; yoghurt; brewer's yeast. Spreading agents for dry skin include: brewer's yeast or Fuller's earth mixed with a little wheatgerm or other oil; 1 egg yolk to 1 teaspoon of honey; mashed fresh peach or avocado or banana. Comfrey leaf juice on its own also makes a soothing face pack for dry skin. For normal skin use one of the following: puréed apple and honey; wheatgerm or oatmeal and honey; egg white and kaolin or Fuller's earth; dried baking yeast.

Hair rinses After shampooing, rinse the hair several times in a warm herbal infusion. Use sage and rosemary for dark hair, chamomile and yarrow for fair hair.

Herbal baths Either put herbs in a piece of muslin (cheese-cloth) made into a bag and hang it from the hot tap so that hot water flows through it, or add 1 litre (1¾ pints) of a strong herbal infusion to the water.

Perfumery

Pot-pourris are a mixture of dried sweet-smelling flower petals, aromatic herbs and spices, and sometimes essential oils and spirits. Moist pot-pourris, usually made with partly dried flowers, orange peel and spirit, are best kept in a closed container, such as a china pomander. Dry pot-pourris are made with completely dried ingredients. A fixative is used to blend the fragrances together and to help retain the scents. Common salt is the usual fixative for moist pot-pourris; orris root and gum benzoin are more often used in dry ones, and have a scent of their own. The ingredients are mixed together and 'cured' by being stored in a sealed container and shaken frequently over a period of about 6 weeks. They are then ready for use.

Herb cushions are used to calm the nerves, induce sleep and soothe headaches, and may be made quite small or pillow-size to sleep on. Stuff a cushion cover with crumbled herbs, adding a few drops of vodka or rose or lavender oil for a sleep pillow, to prevent the herbs crackling inside it. To make a herb sachet for perfuming cupboards, use a cotton lawn bag filled with strong-smelling herbs. To repel moths, use thyme, mint, woodruff, rosemary, sage or marjoram.

Cooking with herbs

There are no firm rules about cooking with herbs; choosing which herbs to use in a particular dish and in what amounts is largely a matter of personal taste. In all but a few dishes, herbs should be used to enhance rather than overpower the flavour of the other ingredients. The exceptions to this are dishes in which the flavour of the herb is intended to be dominant. Soups of parsley, sorrel, dill or garlic, sauces and marinades for fish, made with dill or fennel, and herb flans and omelettes are some examples. Herb butters and mayonnaises, some sorbets, and herbs mixed with soft cheese for dips or spreads are also made with larger quantities of herbs. One tablespoon of fresh herbs or $1/4$-$1/2$ tablespoon of dried is usually enough in a dish for four people.

Parsley or sorrel or watercress soup: 1 onion, finely chopped, 50g/2oz/$1/4$ cup butter, 1 large potato, peeled and diced, 900ml/1$1/2$ pints/3$3/4$ cups chicken stock, salt, black pepper, grated nutmeg to taste, 2 good handfuls parsley, sorrel or watercress, 150ml/$1/4$ pint/$2/3$ cup thin (light) cream.
Melt the butter in a saucepan and cook the onion it it until soft. Add the potatoes, stock and seasoning and simmer until the potatoes are cooked. Remove from the heat and add the parsley, sorrel or watercress. Puree in a blender until smooth, then return to the pan and reheat without boiling. Stir in the cream just before serving. This soup may also be served chilled.

Garlic soup: 1 large bulb garlic, broken into cloves and peeled, 2 tablespoons olive oil, 900ml/1$1/2$ pints/3$3/4$ cups chicken stock, pinch of sage, thyme and cayenne pepper, salt, 3 egg yolks, parsley or chives to garnish.
Stew the cloves in the olive oil over a gentle heat for about 10 minutes. Add all ingredients except the egg yolks, bring to the boil and simmer for 20-30 minutes. Discard the cloves. Whisk the egg yolks, then slowly add some of the hot broth to them, stirring constantly. Pour this mixture back into the broth, still stirring, and heat through gently without boiling until it thickens. Serve garnished with chives.

The culinary use of herbs

	Cheese dishes	Egg dishes	Fish dishes	Garnishes (food)	Garnishes (drink)	Meat, poultry and game dishes	Preserves	Puddings and sweet dishes	Salads and salad dressings	Sauces	Soups and stocks	Stuffings	Vegetables	Wines, beers
ANGELICA				●	●		●	●						●
ANISE			●	●			●	●	●				●	●
BASIL	●	●		●		●			●	●	●	●	●	
BAY			●	●		●		●		●	●		●	
BERGAMOT				●	●	●			●					
BORAGE	●	●		●	●				●					
CARAWAY	●					●			●	●			●	●
CHERVIL	●	●	●	●		●			●	●			●	
CHIVES	●	●	●	●		●			●				●	
COMFREY	●								●					
CORIANDER	●		●					●		●			●	●
CUMIN	●					●	●						●	●
DILL	●	●	●	●		●			●	●	●			
ELDER							●	●						●
FENNEL		●	●	●		●		●	●	●	●	●	●	
GARLIC	●		●			●			●	●	●	●	●	
HOP				●			●						●	●
HORSERADISH		●	●			●			●	●				
HYSSOP				●							●			
JUNIPER						●				●		●		●
LAVENDER						●								
LEMON BALM			●	●	●	●		●	●		●			
LEMON VERBENA			●		●	●		●						
LOVAGE						●			●	●	●			
MARIGOLD				●			●	●	●		●			●
MARJORAM	●	●	●	●		●			●	●	●	●	●	
MARSHMALLOW									●			●		
MINT	●	●		●	●	●	●	●	●	●	●		●	
NASTURTIUM				●					●					
PARSLEY		●	●	●		●			●	●	●	●	●	●
PURSLANE	●	●							●		●		●	
ROSE				●			●	●		●				●
ROSEMARY		●	●		●	●	●	●		●	●	●	●	●
SAGE	●	●		●		●	●		●	●	●		●	
SALAD BURNET	●		●						●	●	●			
SAVORY		●	●			●			●	●	●	●	●	
SORREL		●	●			●			●	●	●	●	●	
SOUTHERNWOOD								●	●					
SWEET CICELY				●	●			●	●		●		●	
TARRAGON	●	●	●	●	●	●	●		●	●	●	●	●	
THYME	●	●	●			●		●		●	●	●	●	
WATERCRESS		●	●	●					●	●	●			
WOODRUFF				●	●									●
YARROW	●									●				

Herbal oils and vinegars These are useful for making salad dressings and marinades. Herbs such as basil, bay, garlic, marjoram, savory, tarragon and thyme are all suitable. Put a few sprigs of the chosen herb (or a mixture) into a bottle of oil or vinegar, and leave for two weeks, shaking daily.

Herb butters Basil, chervil, chives, dill, garlic, mint, parsley, tarragon and lemon thyme are all good in herb butters. Pound together (or mix in a blender) 75g/3oz/6 tablespoons of butter and 3 tablespoons of herbs. Add salt, pepper and lemon juice to taste, blending thoroughly.

Bouquet garni Used in many dishes, a bouquet garni consists of two sprigs each of parsley and thyme, a sprig of marjoram, and a bay leaf. These are either tied together with cotton thread or put inside a muslin (cheesecloth) bag.

Herb teas Many herbs may be made into refreshing teas, drunk either hot or iced, with or without honey or sugar, but always without milk. Herb teas are infusions (see page 22); the best-known ones are chamomile, peppermint, lemon balm, rose hip, marjoram, elderflower, sage and thyme.

Crystallized herbs Angelica, borage, lemon balm, mint and the flowers of many other herbs may be crystallized, for use as decorations on cakes, puddings and sweets. To crystallize herb leaves, dip them first in beaten egg white and then in granulated sugar, and dry them in a very cool oven on a wire cake rack. When they are crisp, allow to cool before storing them in an airtight container. They will only keep for a few days. To crystallize flowers, boil them in a sugar syrup for a minute or two before drying them in an oven.
For crystallized or candied angelica, use young stems and stalks cut into 10cm (4in) lengths. Boil them in salted water until tender, then peel off their outer skin before rinsing the stalks in cold water. Then boil them in sugar syrup — 450g (1lb) of sugar to 280ml (½ pint) water to 450g (1lb) of angelica — for 10 minutes; remove and drain them for 3 or 4 days, then repeat the process in the same syrup, again draining them on a wire rack for a few days. Coat the stalks in sugar and store in airtight containers, where they will keep for some time.

A-Z of common herbs

Angelica (European angelica, garden angelica)
UMBELLIFERAE *Angelica archangelica*
Description A large biennial or perennial plant growing up to 2m (6ft) high in its second year. Native to northern Europe and Asia, where it is found in damp meadows, on river banks and in coastal areas. Stems hollow, grooved, bright green, tinged with reddish-brown at the base and blue near the top. Leaves large, finely toothed, divided into many leaflets arranged in groups of three, growing from dilated sheaths that surround the stems. Flowers tiny, greenish-white or cream massed in large umbels from June to August. Fruit flattish and oblong, and composed of two yellow winged seeds. The whole plant is sweetly scented. The stalks, rootstock, leaves and seeds may all be used.
Cultivation and propagation Sow late summer to mid-autumn in light rich soil and partial shade, in the open ground where it is to flower. Most suitable for the back of a border because of its size. Thin out the seedlings when they

are large enough to handle easily to 15cm (6in) apart. Though a true biennial, angelica will behave as a perennial and continue to grow for a number of years if the flower-heads are not allowed to form. Sometimes flowers do not appear until the fourth year and the roots and stems become bigger, but also tougher. If it is allowed to flower, self-sown seedlings will ensure continuity.

Medicinal Angelica tea made from the leaves and stems calms nerves and reduces tension. Also good for coughs, colds, flatulence, to stimulate appetite, relieve indigestion. A pleasant drink to take after a heavy meal. NB Not to be taken by diabetics. Fresh leaves, crushed and used in a poultice, relieve tightness in the chest, gout and rheumatism. A decoction of the root makes a beneficial skin lotion.

Cosmetic A muslin (cheesecloth) bag full of the fresh leaves added to the water makes a relaxing bath. Use the dried leaves or chopped root in pot-pourris. To perfume a room, burn the seeds and dried roots in front of an open fire. This was common practice until the 18th century.

Culinary Use young stems or leafstalks for crystallizing (candied) angelica, for cakes and garnishing sweet dishes. Also to flavour jams and jellies. Cook leaf stalks with rhubarb, gooseberries or plums to reduce acidity and save sugar. Leaves in wine cups and fruit drinks for a muscatel flavour. Angelica syrup can be diluted to make a refreshing drink or used in winter fruit salads.

Anise (Aniseed, anise plant, common anise)
UMBELLIFERAE *Pimpinella anisum*

Description A small annual plant growing up to 45cm (18in) high. Native to the Mediterranean region and widely grown commercially for its seed (aniseed) which is used as a flavouring in drinks. Stems round, hollow, grooved, branched. Leaves finely serrated, heart-shaped at the base of the plant and finely divided further up. Flowers tiny, white, in compound umbels during July and August. Seeds small and crescent-shaped with a little tail, ripening during August and September. The seeds have a sweet flavour not unlike that of liquorice.

Cultivation and propagation Sow early summer after danger from frost is past in light, well-drained soil in a sunny, sheltered position. Sow in flowering position or transplant seedlings when very small. Thin to 15cm (6in) apart. Gather the seedheads in early autumn and complete drying process indoors. Because of its long tap root anise is not suitable for container or indoor growing.

Medicinal Aniseed tea sweetened with honey is good for the digestion and insomnia, as is a tea made from equal parts anise, fennel and caraway. Chew the seeds to cure hiccups. Anise water promotes milk production in nursing mothers.
Cosmetic A face pack made from ground aniseed will fade freckles. Ground aniseed can be used in pot-pourris.
Culinary Use fresh leaves as a garnish and in salads of both vegetables and fruit. The seeds are good with cooked carrots and cabbage. Both leaves and seeds go well with shellfish. Use the seeds in breads, rolls, cakes, biscuits, sweet pastry, soft cheeses and milk puddings, pickles and sweets.
Basil (common basil, St Josephwort)
LABIATAE *Ocimum basilicum* (sweet basil), *Ocimum minimum* (bush basil)
Description Both annual plants native to India. Sweet basil grows to 30-60cm (12-24in) high, bush basil to only

15cm (6in) high. Both are similar in appearance except that the latter is bushier in habit with smaller leaves and flowers. Stems bushy, branched, reddish. Leaves oval with smooth or slightly toothed edges, 2-7cm (1-3in) long, dark green, often with a purplish tinge. Flowers two-lipped, usually white, but may be pale red in some varieties, blooming in racemes from June to September. (A popular hybrid form, opal basil, has dark purple-bronze leaves and pink flowers). Flavour is clove-like, though sweet basil is preferred for drying because of its larger leaves.

Cultivation and propagation Sow early summer after danger of frost is past, in light rich soil in a sunny, sheltered position, out of doors. Alternatively, sow in pots indoors or under glass in April and plant out at the end of May, after hardening off. Do not overwater seedlings because of their liability to damping-off disease. Transplant to 20cm (8in) apart and, when they are established, pinch out their growing tips to encourage bushiness, and use these in cooking. Bush basil makes an ideal container plant because of its compact habit, and during the winter months may be taken indoors where it will provide more fresh leaves for use over a longer growing period. Cutting the tops regularly (these are the most tender) helps the plant keep its shape.

Medicinal An infusion of basil is good for gastric and

intestinal complaints, including stomach cramps, vomiting, flatulence, constipation, and lack of appetite. Also recommended for headaches. Take for a cough sweetened with honey. The dried, powdered leaves may be taken as snuff to clear the nose and relieve headache.

Cosmetic Dried basil and oil of basil may be used in pot-pourris. Dried leaves may be used in herbal bath bags and in bath vinegars.

Culinary Best known for its affiliation with tomatoes, both in hot tomato sauces, soups and purees, and in tomato salads. Also combines well with egg, mushroom and pasta dishes and is good in potato and rice salads. Use fresh leaves in salads and salad dressings, savoury vinegar, and with fish, poultry, pork and veal. The flavour of the leaves tends to increase when they are cooked.

Bay (sweet bay, bay laurel, true laurel, Roman laurel, Grecian laurel, Indian bay)

LAURACEAE *Laurus nobilis*

Description A perennial evergreen tree growing up to 10-13m (30-40ft), but very slow-growing. Native to the Mediterranean. Leaves aromatic, leathery, smooth, shiny dark green above and paler underneath, about 2-7cm (1-3in) long and with pronounced venation, oval, tapering to a point at both ends, and sometimes with wavy edges. Flowers creamy-white, blooming in the leaf-axils during April and May, developing later into dark purple berries.

Cultivation and propagation Container-grown plants are

readily available from garden-centres and florists. Cuttings of young half-ripened shoots taken in July or August may root with some bottom heat, but are not easy to strike, so take many more cuttings than required, as some will fail. Ordinary soil, preferably in a tub or other container in a sheltered spot, kept well watered for the first month and afterwards if the weather is dry. Top-dress occasionally with well-rotted manure or bone-meal. Vulnerable to severe frosts, so when these are likely bring the tree indoors. Suitable for clipping into a formal shape: if encouraged to grow on one central stem it makes an elegant standard tree. Snip off lateral roots or suckers and round the top into a ball shape. Leaves may be picked throughout the year, and surplus leaves are easily dried but should not be kept for longer than two years as they lose much of their flavour. Good-quality dried leaves are unbroken, supple and pale green; brownish, brittle ones are old and of poor quality.

Medicinal Use bay oil, pressed from leaves and berries, in salves for rheumatism, bruises and skin complaints. Fruit and leaves also improve digestion and stimulate appetite. A decoction of fruit or leaves, made into a paste with honey or syrup, may be applied to the chest for colds. Drink an infusion of the leaves for headaches.

Cosmetic Use as an ingredient in moist pot-pourris made with cologne. Boil with rosemary, lavender, mint and lemon peel and add the resulting water to the bath.

Culinary Use leaves with parsley and thyme to make a *bouquet garni* to flavour many dishes. Add a bay leaf to the water when poaching fish, use them in marinades, soups, stews, casseroles and when making stock. Also valuable in pâtés, stuffings and curries. Store a leaf or two in a jar of rice and add to a rice or milk pudding for a delicious flavour. Always add bay leaves at the beginning of cooking so that they have time to impart their flavour, and remove before serving. Fresh leaves make an attractive garnish for cold sweet and savoury dishes.

Bergamot (bee balm, oswego tea, scarlet monarda, Indian plume, blue balm, high balm, low balm, mountain balm, mountain mint)

LABIATAE *Monarda didyma*

Description A perennial plant up to 90cm (36in) high, found in moist soils in North America, where the Oswego

Indians used it to make the tea that bears their name. Also called bee balm because bees are strongly attracted to its heady scent. Stem square, hairy. Leaves oval, serrated, from 7-15cm (3-6in) long. Flowers scarlet in solitary terminal heads from July to September. Whole plant fragrant, with flowers full of honey and leaves combining the flavours of lemon, mint and rosemary. NB Oil of bergamot comes not from this plant but from a citrus tree, the bergamot orange. The flavour of the two plants is similar, hence this herb's common name.

Cultivation and propagation Plant roots of bergamot in February, cuttings in July. Rich moist soil in shade or partial shade, spacing the plants 60cm (24in) apart, with the roots buried deeply and firmly so that they do not work themselves up to the surface where they will dry out. Showy flowers make this an ideal herb for the herbaceous border; also grows well in a container if kept watered. Water young plants well and established plants in dry weather. Top-dress surrounding soil with well-rotted poultry manure in May. The roots tend to run and the clumps of growth can become bare in the centre so they should be lifted and divided every two years or so and the dead centre discarded. Gather leaves for drying before the plant flowers.

Medicinal Use fresh or dried leaves and flowers to make a soothing tea with a sedative effect, or add to hot milk for the same purpose. Tea also relieves nausea, vomiting and flatulence, and soothes a sore throat.

Cosmetic Use dried leaves and flowers to give colour and fragrance to pot-pourris. Essence of bergamot may be used in herb pillows.

Culinary The chopped flowers and leaves add flavour and colour to green salads, fruit and wine cups. Earwigs like the flowers, so float them in water before use to force the insects out. Leaves go well with pork. Both leaves and flowers dry well and keep their colour throughout the winter.

Borage (bee bread, herb of gladness, burrage, cool tankard, bugloss, common bugloss)

BORAGINACEAE *Borago officinalis*

Description An annual plant up to 60cm (24in) high, native to the Mediterranean, but now found wild throughout Europe. Stem hollow, bristly, branched and spreading, strong-growing. Leaves greyish-green, bristly, oval or oblong, the basal ones forming a rosette and the others growing alternately, on stem and branches. Flowers vivid blue or purplish, sometimes white, star-shaped, in loose racemes from May/June to August, or sometimes longer. Flowers, stems and leaves all have a fresh cucumber flavour.

Cultivation and propagation Sow March to April in rather poor soil, preferably of chalk or sand, in well-drained, sunny position. Sow seed 5cm (2in) deep and 60cm (24in) apart where the plants are to flower, putting two or three seeds at each station and thinning to leave the strongest growing (borage does not transplant well). Seeds germinate quickly and plants are fully grown in 5 to 6 weeks. Alternatively, seed sown in September will overwinter as rosettes and flower the following May. Borage seeds itself freely and will come up again.

Medicinal An infusion of the dried flowers or leaves is said to be good for reducing fever and for restoring vitality during convalescence, and as a general tonic. It seems to have a

calming effect; also good for liver and kidney troubles, and as a laxative. The leaves and seeds stimulate the flow of milk in nursing mothers.

Cosmetic Fresh leaves used in a face pack for dry skin.

Culinary Use the flowers to garnish any sweet or savoury dish. Add finely chopped young leaves to soft cheese or yoghurt for a cucumber flavour, also to salads and egg dishes. Decorate wine cups and cold fruit drinks with leaves and flowers. Flowers may be crystallized.

Caraway

UMBELLIFERAE *Carum carvi*

Description A biennial or perennial plant up to 60cm (24in) high, cultivated and found wild in northern USA, Europe and Asia. Stem hollow, furrowed, angular, branched. Root white, carrot-shaped. Leaves deeply incised, feathery. Flowers small, white or yellow in compound umbels with rays of unequal length, in May and June. Fruit dark brown, oblong, flattened, containing two seeds, bursting open when ripe. Grown for seeds and roots only; these have an anise-like flavour.

Cultivation and propagation Sow April/May or autumn in light, well-drained soil in a sunny spot, thinning to 20cm (8in) apart when the seedlings are big enough to handle. Germinates quickly. May be grown in containers and window boxes if it has enough sun to ripen the seeds. In the first year the plants will reach about 20cm (8in) high. Seed is ripe for collection the year after sowing — care is required in this as the plant scatters it very easily if disturbed. When fruit begins to ripen at the end of July/August, and before any of it has burst open, cut down the stems to the ground and hang up to dry. When completely dry rub seeds from the stalks and put in jars. Dig up roots for eating after harvesting seeds.

Medicinal Chew the seeds or use in an infusion to help the digestion and appetite. Use caraway for colic in infants and to settle the stomach and relieve flatulence. Caraway promotes the onset of menstruation, relieves uterine cramps and promotes lactation.

Cosmetic Add crushed seeds to pot-pourris and to muslin bags with cloves, cinnamon, mace and dried rose petals to perfume clothes and linen.

Culinary Use small amounts of seed to flavour pork, duck, liver and vegetables such as cabbage, cauliflower and potatoes. Also in cakes, biscuits (cookies), bread, buns, and sprinkled on potato cakes. Use ground in sweets and in cream cheese.

Chamomile (German chamomile, scented mayweed, wild chamomile, chamomilla)

COMPOSITAE *Matricaria recutita*

Description An annual up to 40cm (16in) high, native to southern Europe, found along roadsides and in fields. Stem round, downy, hollow, furrowed, either growing along the ground with just the tips turning upwards, or upright. Leaves pale green, deeply incised, feathery, without stalks. Flowers consist of a prominent yellow disk surrounded by white petals which turn back towards the stalk, blooming in June and July, smelling of apples.

Cultivation and propagation Sow early spring in well-drained soil in a dry sunny position where it is to flower. (It is said that where chamomile grows the plants in the garden will be healthier). Mix sand with the tiny seeds to make sowing more even, keep well watered until the leaves

appear. Thin to 15cm (6in) apart when 5cm (2in) high. Harvest the flowerheads when the petals have turned back but before they turn brown at the back near the calyx. Dry them on paper in a cool, airy place and store in screwtop jars. If flowers are left to go to seed, chamomile will seed itself freely and come up again.

Medicinal An infusion of chamomile (3 or 4 fresh or 5 or 6 dried flowers to 1 cup water) makes a good mouthwash for use after dental treatment and for toothache. A soothing tea for stomach upsets and indigestion. Use chamomile as a wash or compress for inflammation, rashes and other skin problems. When used as a facial steam it relieves a heavy head cold and asthma in children. Use in a sitz bath to help haemorrhoids, and as a foot- or hand-bath for sweaty feet or hands. For haemorrhoids and wounds, make the flowers into a salve.

Cosmetic Infusion well known as a herbal rinse for fair hair. As a face wash or lotion to keep skin soft and supple; added to face packs with yarrow, carrot and egg white for oily skin. Use with rosemary, bay, thyme and basil in herbal sachets for the bath. Dried flowers in pot-pourris.

Roman Chamomile (common chamomile, maythen, manzanilla, bowman, garden chamomile, ground apple, low chamomile, whig plant)

COMPOSITAE *Chamaemelum nobile*

Description A perennial up to 30cm (12in) high, native to Europe, found in dry fields and on cultivated ground. Appearance similar to that of German chamomile except for its more prostrate habit and the fact that the flower petals do not bend back; some varieties have double flowers. Prostrate habit makes it the most suitable for paths and lawns.

Cultivation and propagation Roman chamomile is best as a lawn. To make a chamomile lawn, sow the seed in boxes and plant out when 5cm (2in) high in staggered rows 10cm (4in) apart — 80 plants are needed to the square metre. Lawn must not be allowed to flower: in the first summer clip with shears and use the mower with the blades set high in subsequent summers. Must be hand weeded as the chemicals in weedkillers and other lawn dressings will kill the chamomile.

Uses As for German chamomile, when allowed to flower.

Chervil
UMBELLIFERAE *Anthriscus cerefolium*
Description An annual plant up to 50cm (20in) high, native to southeast Europe and southwest Asia. Stem round, finely grooved, branched. Leaves light green, finely divided, fernlike. Flowers small, white, growing in compound umbels from May to July. Seeds elongated, segmented, ripening in August and September. Mild, anise-like flavour of leaves means generous use necessary. Use leaves only.

Cultivation and propagation Sow from March to late summer, a few seeds at a time for a succession of fresh leaves and because plants tend to bolt and burst into flower quickly. Leaves of little use after plant flowers. Well-drained, moist soil in partial shade. Can be container-grown. Germinates quickly. Thin seedlings to 15cm (6in) apart. Can be used when the plants are about 10cm (4in) high, about 6-8 weeks after sowing. Snip off close to the root and the plants will grow again to provide a second cut. Let some early plants run to seed for sowing later. Save seed from late-flowering plants for the following year. Prolong growing season by using cloches.
Medicinal An infusion of the leaves promotes digestion, relieves flatulence and catarrh, and is said to lower blood

pressure. Apply juice from the fresh leaves to stings, bites and abcesses. A compress of fresh leaves reduces bruising.
Cosmetic Use infusion of leaves as a cleansing lotion.
Culinary Traditionally used in the *fines herbes* mixture of French cuisine. Particularly good used fresh in chervil soup. Add to butter sauces for use with delicate vegetables and as a garnish.

Chives

LILIACEAE *Allium schoenoprasum*

Description A hardy perennial plant up to 30-40cm (12-15in) high, probably native to the Mediterranean region but now widespread throughout Europe, Asia and North America, growing alongside waterways. Leaves narrow, hollow, cylindrical, grasslike, closed at the top and dilated to surround the stem at the bottom. Naked stems emerge from clumps of tiny bulbs to bear a spherical terminal cluster of pink or pale mauve flowers in June and July. Leaves have a mild onion flavour.

Cultivation and propagation Sow spring, but slow to germinate. Easier to divide clumps of established bulbs in spring or autumn and plant in small groups of bulbs 20cm (8in) apart. Light, rich, damp soil in sunny position. Water well in times of drought. Makes a good border for the herb garden; may also be grown in containers and indoors if

given a liquid feed every 2 weeks to prevent the tops of the leaves turning brown. Grow several clumps for a succession of new growth and use the plants in rotation. Flavour better if not allowed to flower. Can be harvested all year round: cut leaves off to about 2cm (1 in) above the ground and chop up with scissors. Lift and divide clumps every 3 or 4 years, in autumn.

Medicinal Chopped fresh chives sprinkled over food stimulate appetite and promote digestion. Mildly laxative.

Culinary Chopped fresh chives are good sprinkled over salads, soups, chicken and veal, cooked vegetables, particularly potatoes, and egg dishes. Lose flavour when cooked so add at last minute. Chives have an affinity with cream cheese. Bulbs may be used like spring onions or pickled in white wine vinegar.

Comfrey (blackwort, bruisewort, common comfrey, knitbone, boneset, knitback, ass ear, consound, healing herb, gum plant, salsify, slippery root, wallwort)
BORAGINACEAE *Symphytum officinale*
Description A perennial plant 60-90cm (24-36in) tall found in moist soils in North America and Europe. Rootstock large and spreading, black outside, fleshy and whitish inside, containing a glutinous, almost tasteless juice. Stem angular, hairy. Leaves large, coarse, bristly, oval but

tapering to a point, the basal ones tongue-shaped. Flowers mauve or creamy-white, bell-like, growing in lop-sided curved spikes from May to August.

Cultivation and propagation Sow early spring in any moist soil, in flowering position, thinning to 30-45cm (12-18in) apart. Most useful as a background or screening plant. Not suitable for container-growing, because of large root system. May also be propagated by division of roots in spring, but once established will seed itself. Young leaves may be picked for use throughout growing season, and the roots dug up in autumn. Useful composting plant.

Medicinal A decoction of the root and leaves helps ease coughs and other bronchial ailments; its use as a gargle and mouthwash will help throat inflammations, hoarseness, and bleeding gums. Apply a poultice of roots and/or leaves for bronchitis, pleurisy, bruises, swellings, insect bites, rheumatic pains and painful joints, and to help heal scars. Cotton wool dipped in an infusion of leaves and applied to affected area will soothe cuts and abrasions and help them heal. A hot decoction of the root applied to a stye will relieve the pain and bring it to a head.

Cosmetic Add comfrey root to the bathwater for a tonic bath which will soften skin. Use strained juice from pulped leaves as a face pack, and an infusion of the leaves as a lotion for dry skin. Use leaves in a facial steam.

Culinary Use chopped young leaves in salads, or cooked in a cheese sauce, or dipped in batter and deep-fried.

Coriander (Chinese parsley)

UMBELLIFERAE *Coriandrum sativum*

Description An annual plant up to 60cm (24in) high, widespread in North and South America, Europe, and the Mediterranean, having been cultivated for thousands of years. Found wild in waste ground. Stem round, finely grooved. Leaves finely divided, like parsley, the upper ones even finer. Flowers white or pale mauve, in flat compound umbels of 3 to 5 rays, from June to August. Seeds round, brownish, ripening to pale beige. Ripe seeds aromatic, tasting spicy, sage-like.

Cultivation and propagation Sow early spring in light rich soil in full sun, where it is to flower. Thin to 10-15cm (4-6in) apart. Needs as long a growing season as possible to ensure ripening of seeds. In late summer when the seeds

have turned light greyish-brown, cut down the plants and put them in a dry airy place for a few days. When completely dry shake out the seeds and store in screwtop jars; their aroma improves with keeping. Seeds remain fertile for up to 5 years, so save for sowing in following years.

Medicinal An infusion of seeds improves digestion and appetite, and relieves flatulence. Apply externally in an ointment for rheumatism and painful joints.

Cosmetic Use crushed seed infused in rubbing alcohol (1 part seed to 5 parts spirit, kept for 3-4 weeks) as a skin freshener. Use seeds as an ingredient of pot-pourris and herb bags.

Culinary Use crushed seed in a spice mixture for curries. Good in apple pies, cakes, biscuits (cookies), gingerbread, and when making chutney and marmalade. Use whole seed in vegetable dishes, and to flavour soups, sauces and meat dishes.

Cumin

UMBELLIFERAE *Cuminum cyminum*

Description An annual plant 30-60cm (12-24in) tall, native to Egypt and Ethiopia. Stem stiff, grooved and branching. Leaves long, threadlike, deep green. Flowers small, white or pale pink, borne in umbels in June and July. Grown for the seeds which ripen in August, similar to

caraway seeds but larger (0.5cm (¼in) long) with a stronger, warmer flavour.

Cultivation and propagation Sow late spring/early summer outdoors, or indoors under glass with bottom heat in early spring in rich soil in warm, sheltered position in sun. Thin plants to 15cm (6in) apart when they are large enough to handle. With plenty of sun the seeds should be ready for harvesting after 3 or 4 months. Cut down the plants and finish drying them indoors; the seeds have an unpleasant flavour before they are fully ripe.

Medicinal An infusion of the seeds aids digestion.

Culinary Use ground seed as an ingredient of curry powder. Particularly good in lentil soup. Use whole seeds in rye bread, in pickles and chutneys, cakes, biscuits (cookies), and add to the water when cooking cabbage or kidney beans. Mix with cottage cheese and lemon juice for a spread or dip.

Dill (dilly, garden dill)

UMBELLIFERAE *Anethum graveolens*

Description An annual plant up to 90cm (36in) high, native to southern Europe, but now found wild in North and South America and northern Europe. Stem hollow, finely grooved, striped dark green and white with bluish spots. Leaves bluish-green, very finely cut, the base dilating into a sheath surrounding the stem. Flowers tiny, deep yellow, in flat, compound umbels from July to September. Seeds oval, ribbed, flat, brownish. All parts of the plant are aromatic with a slightly sharp yet sweet flavour, similar to but milder than that of fennel. Both leaves and seeds are used.

Cultivation and propagation Sow April to June, every few weeks for a succession of young leaves. Good, well-drained soil in a sunny position where they are to remain. Sow in a drill and thin the seedlings to 30cm (12in) apart. May be container-grown. Grow away from fennel, to avoid confusion between the two, particularly when you harvest the seeds. Use the leaves before the plant flowers. To harvest seeds, cut down plants as they begin to ripen and hang up to dry indoors.

Medicinal Gripe water, made from the seeds, is given to babies for hiccups and to induce sleep. An infusion of the seeds relieves indigestion and stomach upsets, acts as a tranquillizer, and promotes the flow of milk in nursing mothers. Chew the seeds to sweeten the breath.

Cosmetic Dill-seed tea, either drunk or used as a hand rinse, will help to strengthen nails.

Culinary Dill leaves are particularly good in a sauce for fish. Also in salads, and especially with cucumber. Also good with chicken, rabbit and veal, in cream soups, egg dishes and in mayonnaise and mustard. Blend with cream or cottage cheese for a dip or spread. Use whole or ground seeds in herb butters, bean soups, and in pickles, particularly pickled cucumber (dill pickles).

Elder (pipe tree, bore tree, sweet elder, black elder, black-berried European elder, boor tree, bountry, ellanwood, ellhorn, German elder [for European elder]. Black elder, common elder, elderberry, rob elder, sweet elder [for American elder]).

CAPRIFOLIACEAE *Sambucus nigra* (European elder), *Sambucus canadensis* (American elder),

Description A hardy deciduous shrub, the European elder growing up to 7m (22ft) high, the American elder up to 3m (12ft) high. European elder is common in hedgerows and moist, shady places in Europe; American elder is found in damp areas and waste places, particularly in central and eastern USA. Stems covered in rough, brownish-grey bark. Leaves oval, finely serrated, dark green. Flowers small, creamy-white or white, in branching flat-topped clusters,

fragrant, from May to July. Small, spherical, shiny dark purple berries in late summer.

Cultivation and propagation Slow to start from seed. Better to plant young plants in late autumn or early spring before growth starts. Any good garden soil in sun or partial shade. Not suitable for container growing. Prune in late autumn or early spring to prevent undue spreading. To propagate take cuttings of leafless shoots in autumn or by the more difficult method of root division. Not essential in the herb garden as common in the countryside.

Medicinal Green elder ointment (3 parts leaves to 4 parts lard and 2 parts suet, or to 6 parts petroleum jelly, heated together until colour is extracted from the leaves, strained and cooled) is good for chilblains, insect bites and burns. An infusion of the leaves may be used as a diuretic. An infusion of the flowers promotes perspiration and is good for feverish colds, catarrh, and rheumatism, and to calm the nerves. A syrup made from the berries is also good for coughs and colds. An elderflower infusion makes a good compress for acne, spots and boils.

Cosmetic Elderflower water (an infusion) is mildly astringent and makes a good skin cleanser and softener. Apply in a compress for wrinkles, sunburn or freckles, and add to the bath water for a refreshing bath. Good also in a facial steam bath for oily skin.

Culinary Elderflowers make a heady wine, a fragrant sorbet (sherbet), and a good cordial for use as a drink or as a basis for fruit salads. Also good in jams, jellies, vinegars, pancakes and fritters. Berries also used to make wine and other drinks, jams, jellies (good with crab-apples), apple tarts and instead of raisins in other puddings.

NB all parts of American elder can cause poisoning when used fresh, so must be cooked. The berries of European elder must not be eaten raw for the same reason.

Eyebright (red eyebright, euphrasy)
SCROPHULARIACEAE *Euphrasia rostkoviana*
Description An annual plant up to 30cm (12in) high, native to pastures and other grassy areas of Europe and western Asia, and naturalized in some areas of the USA. Stem downy, square. Leaves stiff, oval, deeply cut. Flowers tiny, two-lipped, white streaked with purple or red and yellow, blooming from June to September.

Cultivation and propagation Sow in spring on a grassy patch of ground (the roots feed on the roots of nearby plants), as thinly as possible so that thinning of the plants will not be necessary. If allowed to go to seed it will come up year after year. Not essential in a herb garden as it grows in the wild. Not easy to cultivate.

Medicinal A weak infusion of the fresh leaves and flowers may be used as an eyewash or hot compress (fomentation) to treat inflammation and strain. Eyebright tea acts as a tonic.

Cosmetic Use an infusion of the leaves and flowers as a lotion to soothe the skin around the eyes.

Fennel (fenkel, large fennel, sweet fennel, wild fennel) UMBELLIFERAE *Foeniculum vulgare*

Description A biennial or perennial plant up to 1.5m (5ft) tall, native to the Mediterranean region but found wild elsewhere in Europe and also in the USA. Stem stout, pithy, finely grooved with fine bluish stripes. Leaves finely divided, feathery, the upper ones on broad sheaths that surround the stem, light green when young, becoming darker. Flowers bright yellow, in large compound umbels from July to October. Seeds yellowish-brown, oval, ribbed, with a strong scent and sweet anise-like flavour, stronger than that of the leaves. Whole plant closely resembles dill.

Cultivation and propagation Sow early spring in moist, well-drained good garden soil, preferably chalky, in sun. Thin to 30cm (12in) apart. Self-sown seedlings will appear freely but the main plants can be divided every 3 or 4 years. Use fresh light green leaves. Harvest seeds when hard and a grey-green colour. Cut off seed-heads and complete drying indoors. Florence fennel or finocchio *(F. v. dulce)* is a variety with an edible swollen leaf base like celery. It needs a very long warm growing season and plenty of moisture. Leaves and seeds can be used as for garden fennel; the bulb may be eaten raw or cooked.

Medicinal An infusion of seeds or leaves is a good treatment for tired eyes and inflamed eyelids. Fennel tea promotes the appetite, relieves colic, flatulence and stomach cramps. Also good for coughs and bronchial congestion. The tea is diuretic and a mild laxative, and helps stimulate the flow of milk in nursing mothers. To relieve rheumatism, rub fennel oil on affected areas.

Cosmetic Use an infusion of the leaves as a lotion to refresh the skin and against wrinkles; with yoghurt as a skin cleanser. A strong infusion of fennel mixed with glycerine and arrowroot makes a good hand cream.

Culinary Leaves are good with fish; also in soups and stuffings and with pork. Use in salads and on raw and cooked vegetables, in bread and savoury biscuits (crackers) and in the water used for poaching fish.

Garlic (poor man's treacle)

LILIACEAE *Allium sativum*

Description A perennial bulb of the onion family up to 60cm (24in) high, native to Asia but now established throughout the world. Its underground bulb is composed of a number of bulbets, called cloves, enclosed together in a whitish skin. Stem simple, smooth and round, surrounded at the bottom by tubular leaf sheaths. Leaves long, flat, narrow, green to blue-green. Flowers small, white, usually sterile, in a rounded umbel which is first enclosed in a teardrop-shaped leaf pointing upward, which eventually falls off.

Cultivation and propagation Plant individual cloves in late winter or early spring in rich, friable, moist soil in sunny position, 5cm (2in) deep and 15cm (6in) apart. May be container-grown. Keep well watered in dry weather. In August or September the leaves die down and the plants should be dug up. Dry the bulbs away from sun but in a dry, airy place. Keep largest cloves for planting again.

Medicinal Use juice pressed from the cloves, thinned with water or milk to aid digestion and to treat intestinal infections. Also good for chronic bronchitis and catarrh, if taken regularly. Tincture of garlic lowers blood pressure.

Culinary Use to flavour all savoury dishes, hot or cold. Particularly good with lamb or mutton, inserting slices of the cloves into incisions in the meat before roasting. Also good mashed with butter for garlic bread.

Hop

CANNABACEAE *Humulus lupulus*

Description A vigorous perennial vine up to 6m (20ft) high, found wild climbing over hedges in most parts of Europe. Stem rough, angular. Leaves rough, serrated, with three to five lobes. Flowers yellowish-green, in hanging clusters of five tiny petals each in the male plant, in catkins in the female. Fruit, called hops, from the female flowers only, scaly, cone-like. Only female plants cultivated, for the hops which are dried to make beer and ale.

Cultivation and propagation Sow late spring in rich, well-worked soil in full sun, against a fence, wall or trellis up which they can be trained. Thin seedlings to 15-30cm (6-12in) apart. Keep watered in dry weather and top-dress soil in spring. Can also be propagated by root division in spring. In early autumn gather female flowers for drying and cut down the plant in late autumn.

Medicinal Hops are most commonly used for their calming effect on the nervous system: hop tea is recommended for nervous diarrhoea, insomnia and restlessness. Put crumbled dried hops sprinkled with alcohol into a pillow to aid sleep and to help relieve asthma. For acne, spots and boils, apply a hot poultice of hops to the affected area. NB Hops lose their effectiveness rapidly when stored.

Culinary In summer young hop shoots may be cooked until tender and served as a vegetable with butter and a little lemon juice or a vinaigrette dressing.

Horseradish (mountain radish, red cole)

CRUCIFERAE *Armoracia rusticana*

Description A perennial growing to a height of 60-100cm (24-36in) high, native to southeastern Europe and south west Asia, but naturalized in the rest of Europe since the 12th century. Roots long, white, fleshy, thick, with a hot biting taste. Stem stout, grooved, short. Leaves from base of plant large, floppy, oblong with scalloped edges, smaller stem leaves, characteristic smell when crushed. Flowers small, numerous, white, on a single stem during June and July (does not flower every season).

Cultivation and propagation Sow or plant early spring in well-drained, light rich soil (not clay), deeply dug so roots can grow long and straight, on an open sunny site. Thin seedlings or plant shoots 30cm (12in) apart, or bury roots larger end upwards 5cm (2in) deep. Not suitable for containers. Lift roots every autumn or winter and store in damp sand until required. Save some pieces of root for planting on a fresh site the following spring. Once established it spreads and is hard to eradicate.

Medicinal For bladder infections take 4 tablespoons grated root in wine vinegar sweetened with honey or raw sugar. 15-20 drops of juice taken between meals is useful for colitis and intestinal problems, also (with honey) for bronchial catarrh, coughs and asthma. Contains vitamin C. Use as a poultice for bites, chilblains, stiff muscles and rheumatism.

Culinary A superb sauce for roast beef, but also good with oily or smoked fish. Add to mayonnaise for cold fish, and for cold hard-boiled eggs. Add grated root to salads, especially coleslaw, and to pickled beetroot.

Hyssop

LABIATAE *Hyssopus officinalis*

Description A hardy evergreen perennial plant up to 60cm (24in) high, native to the Mediterranean region and central Asia, but naturalized in western Asia, central Europe and parts of the USA. Stem square, downy, branching, woody at the base. Leaves small, long and pointed, sometimes downy, fragrant. Flowers bluish-purple or deep pink, clustered in leaf axils at tops of stems, very fragrant, blooming from June to October. Whole plant has a spicy, slightly bitter taste, somewhat like mint.

Cultivation and propagation Sow spring in light, well-drained moist soil in sun. Thin seedlings to 60cm (24in) apart. May be container-grown, or clipped into a hedge. Once established, hyssop seeds itself. May also be propagated by taking stem cuttings in spring or by root division in autumn or early spring. Plant near cabbage to help repel cabbage-white butterflies. To use the fresh herb both stalks and leaves can be cut just before plant flowers, but if to be dried, take just the leaves.

Medicinal Drink hyssop tea for catarrh, colds, coughs and chest troubles, and to improve digestion and stimulate appetite. Use crushed leaves on sore muscles and on wounds to prevent infection. Use a decoction as a wash for burns, bruises and as a gargle for a sore throat.

Cosmetic Add dried flowers and leaves to pot-pourris. Use an infusion to bathe tired eyes.

Culinary Add fresh leaves to green salads and vegetable soups. Use fresh or dried herb sparingly with roast duck, goose or pork and in rich pâtés, also in rabbit pies and lamb stews. Also good with pulses. Add to cooked fruit dishes, especially cranberries, peaches and apricots.

Juniper (Hack matack, horse savin)

CUPRESSACEAE *Juniperus communis*

Description An evergreen shrub-like conifer up to 4m (12ft) high, found in dry rocky soil in upland regions of Europe, Asia and North America. Bark brown tinged with red. Leaves needle-like, short and tough, bluish-green with a white stripe above, shiny yellow-green underneath. Flowers small, yellow on male plant, green on female plant, in April to June. Fruit a berry-like cone, green the first year, ripening to blue-black or dark purple the second, with a spicy bitter-sweet taste and a dry, granular texture. Whole plant aromatic, resinous.

Cultivation and propagation Sow spring, in a cold frame to plant outdoors a year later. Easy to grow from seed. Alternatively take stem cuttings from new growth and set in sandy soil under glass in early autumn, for planting out the following spring. Good garden soil in an open, well-drained position. Plant male and female plants next to each other to be certain of producing berries. (Male plants grow more upright than female ones.) To dry berries, pick in September/October and dry in a thin layer in an airy place, in a

temperature not above 35°C (95°F), otherwise the essential oil evaporates.

Medicinal Take juniper berry tea or chew a few berries for indigestion and intestinal cramps, and as a diuretic. Juniper oil in an inhalant vapour bath is useful for bronchitis and lung infections. NB Not to be taken by pregnant women or by those with kidney problems.

Cosmetic Make a stimulating face pack for normal skin from an infusion of young juniper shoots made into a paste with egg white and Fuller's earth or kaolin.

Culinary Crushed berries in stuffings for pork, poultry and game dishes. Four berries can replace a bay leaf in sauces and marinades, and be added to the water when boiling ham or cooking cabbage. Use crushed berries in pâtés.

Lavender

LABIATAE *Lavandula angustifolia* (English lavender);
L. stoechas (French or Spanish lavender); *L. dentata* (Fringed or French lavender)

Description A perennial shrub with many species and varieties, growing from 30-90cm (12-33in) high, native to the western Mediterranean region. Stem grey-green, angular, with flaking bark. Leaves narrow, downy, grey-green,

59

aromatic. Flowers purple, mauve, blue, pink or sometimes white, tubular in spikes at the top of the stem, strongly scented, blooming mid- to late-summer.

Cultivation and propagation Sow spring. Will also grow from cuttings with a heel, taken in spring or autumn, set in sand, and planted out in late autumn for spring cuttings, spring for autumn cuttings. Well-drained soil with a lime content, firmly planted in a sunny sheltered spot. Dwarf forms *(L. angustifolia* and *L. stoechas)* may be container grown or used to edge the herb garden. Larger varieties also good for hedging. Plant out seedlings 75cm (30in) apart for large varieties and 30-40cm (12-16in) apart for dwarf types. May need protection in severe winters, especially from high winds. Prune after flowering to keep a good shape. Tend to become leggy after 4 or 5 years so should be replaced with cuttings. May also be propagated by root division.

Medicinal A few drops of lavender oil taken on a sugar cube or mixed with honey are used for flatulence, migraine, fainting and dizziness. A decoction of leaves is useful for stomach problems, nausea and vomiting. Use an embrocation of oil for muscular stiffness, and as an antiseptic.

Cosmetic Bags of lavender added to bath water are refreshing. With other herbs makes a good facial steam; use an infusion as a skin tonic. Make lavender water with 1 part flowers to 4 parts rubbing alcohol; leave for a month before straining. Use dried lavender flowers in herb cushions and pot-pourris, and in muslin (cheesecloth) bags to repel moths.

Culinary Use sparingly with other herbs for roast and grilled meat. Put a few flowerheads into sugar to scent it.

Lemon balm (balm, sweet balm, balm mint, bee balm, blue balm, cure-all, dropsy plant, garden balm, melissa)
LABIATAE *Melissa officinalis*

Description A perennial bushy plant up to 90cm (33in) high, native to the eastern Mediterranean region but now found in southern Europe, western Asia and some parts of the USA, growing wild in fields and along roadsides. Stem square, hairy, upright, branched. Leaves oval with roughly serrated edges, somewhat hairy, with pronounced venation, light green, sometimes with gold flecks in variegated varieties, lemon-scented. Flowers small, white, pale pink or pale blue, growing in leaf axils in July and August.

Cultivation and propagation Sow spring, to plant out in autumn for harvest the following year. Slow to germinate,

so best grown from stem cuttings taken in spring or autumn. Ordinary, moist soil in sun or light shade. Plant out 30cm (12in) apart. Spreads rapidly so cut back to keep it a compact shape. May also be propagated by root division in spring or autumn. Suitable for growing in containers. Leaves dry well and should be harvested in cool, dry weather and dried in shade.

Medicinal Use balm tea to relieve indigestion and flatulence, chronic bronchial catarrh, menstrual cramps and for headaches and dizziness during pregnancy. Its calming effects make it useful for nervous problems and insomnia. Use crushed leaves as a poultice for sores and insect bites.

Cosmetic Use dried leaves in pot-pourris and herb pillows.

Culinary Use as a substitute for lemon, in generous quantities because of its mild flavour. Make lemon tea by adding leaves to pot with Indian tea, and use in stuffings for lamb and pork. Also good spread over chicken before roasting. Substitute for parsley in a sauce for fish.

Lemon verbena (herb Louisa, lemon-scented verbena)
VERBENACEAE *Aloysia triphylla*
Description A tender perennial shrub up to 1.5m (5ft) tall,

native to South America. Stem woody, branching. Leaves long, narrow, pointed, crinkled, in groups of 3 or 4, smelling strongly of lemon. Flowers tiny, white or mauve, carried in pointed spikes from July to September.

Cultivation and propagation Plant stem cuttings of an established plant at any time during growing season. Ordinary to poor, well-drained soil in a warm sheltered position, preferably against a sunny wall. Needs winter protection if grown outdoors. May be container grown or potted up and taken indoors or put in a greenhouse for the winter. Pot-grown plants need plenty of water in summer, little in winter. Prune in February to within 30cm (12in) of the base of the plant and pinch out tops of shoots during growing season to stop it becoming straggly. Save shoots for drying: the dried leaves retain their scent well.

Medicinal Drink lemon verbena tea after a heavy meal to aid digestion, and to aid sleep. An infusion used nightly for cleaning teeth is good for gums and helps prevent tooth decay.

Cosmetic Add an infusion of the leaves to the bath water. Use a decoction of the leaves as a lotion to cleanse skin. Use dried leaves in herb cushions, in sachets to scent clothes and linen, and in pot-pourris.

Culinary Use sparingly in fruit salads, jellies and drinks. Try in homemade ice cream for a strong fragrant flavour, and to flavour milk puddings, cakes and sweet sauces.

Lovage (Italian lovage, European lovage, lavose)
UMBELLIFERAE *Levisticum officinale*

Description A hardy perennial up to 2m (6½ft) tall, native to southern Europe and western Asia but cultivated in central and northern Europe since the Middle Ages and found wild throughout the Continent. Root short, thick, strong, fleshy. Stem straight, round, hollow, branched near the top. Leaves large, deeply divided, on long stems, those near the top of the plant smaller, stalkless, thin and narrow. Flowers small, pale greenish-yellow, in compound umbels from June to August. Seeds ridged, oblong, brown. All parts of the plant can be used, and have a strong yeasty flavour and aroma similar to that of celery.

Cultivation and propagation Sow early summer in rich moist soil in sun or partial shade, in drills thinned to 60cm (24in) apart, at the back of the herb border. Make sure seed is ripe before sowing. If the ground is kept well cultivated a plant will last for several years and if allowed to set seed will self-sow easily. To ensure plenty of young leaves, cut off at least the early flowers. Cut the foliage for use frequently but leave the young leaves at the centre. Can also be propagated by division in spring or autumn.

Medicinal An infusion of the root, leaves or seeds acts as a diuretic, stimulates appetite and relieves flatulence. NB Not to be taken by those with kidney problems or in pregnancy.

Cosmetic Use the root or leaves to perfume the bath water.
Culinary Use leaves sparingly in soups, stocks and casseroles. Young leaves and stalks may be cooked as a vegetable, with white sauce. Add leaves in any recipe where a celery flavour is required. Young stems may be candied like angelica.
Marigold (pot marigold, golds, Mary gowles, Mary bud, garden marigold, marygold, ruddes, holigold, calendula)
COMPOSITAE *Calendula officinalis*
Description A hardy annual plant up to 75cm (30in) high, native to India but cultivated for centuries in Europe. Not to be confused with more common African and French marigolds. Stem angular, hairy, branched. Leaves hairy,

oblong, pointed at the base, with widely spaced teeth and growing directly from the main stem. Flowers large, bright orange or yellow, sometimes with a centre darker than the petals, in single terminal heads, from June to October or later.

Cultivation and propagation Sow spring or autumn in light rich soil in sun, thinning seedlings to 45-60cm (18-24in) apart. Good as border edging or as container plant. Seeds itself freely if a few of the early flowers are left on the plant to ripen fully by late summer. Scatter the seed in autumn

where they are to flower the following year. Prolong flowering season by cutting off flowerheads as they fade. Leaves can be gathered for use at any time.

Medicinal A tea of the fresh or dried flowers (petals or whole heads) relieves gastro-intestinal problems such as ulcers, cramps, colitis and diarrhoea, and is also good for poor circulation, varicose veins, fever, and skin problems such as boils. An oil or ointment made from the flowers is good for sunburn, acne, ulcers and helps scars to fade.

Cosmetic Use an infusion of the flower petals as a bath for tired swollen feet, and as a lotion for cleansing the skin. Use in a tonic bath to revitalize skin after cold winter months, in a facial steam, and mixed with almond oil (left in a sunny

place for 3 or 4 weeks, then strained) for dry, rough hands.
Culinary Use chopped petals to give colour and flavour to
soups, stews, salads, cheese and egg dishes, and as a
substitute for saffron with rice. Add to custards and puddings, cakes and buns. Use petals as a food colouring by
simmering them in milk (1 part petals to 2 parts milk) until
soft, and liquidizing till smooth. Petals retain colour well
when dried.

Marjoram· (knotted marjoram [for sweet marjoram];
oregano, mountain mint, winter marjoram, wintersweet
[for wild marjoram])

LABIATAE *Origanum onites* (pot marjoram), *Origanum
majorana* (sweet marjoram), *Origanum vulgare* (wild
marjoram)

Description Pot marjoram: a perennial plant up to 60cm
(24in) high, native to the Mediterranean region but found
wild throughout Europe and cultivated in the US. Stem
square, branched, downy. Leaves small, rounded, serrated, hairy. Flowers small, white or pink in dense terminal
clusters from late summer to mid-autumn. Golden m. *(O.
onites aureum)* is a variety with golden leaves in spring and
early summer, turning green later in the growing season
and reverting to golden the following year. Both have strong
spicy, sweet flavour.

Sweet marjoram: a perennial plant up to 45cm (18in) high,

native to North Africa and the Middle East but cultivated in central and northern Europe and North America. Stem square, branched, downy with grey hairs. Leaves small, elliptic, with greyish down. Flowers small, white or pink in spherical clusters, 3-5 per cluster, from late summer to mid-autumn. Has best flavour for cooking.

Wild marjoram: a perennial plant up to 75cm (30in) high, native to Europe and the Middle East and cultivated in the USA. Stem square, branched, downy, purplish. Leaves oval, pointed, dotted with small depressions. Flowers purple, two-lipped, in terminal clusters from late summer to mid-autumn. Has strongest taste of the three.

Cultivation and propagation Pot m: grow in areas too cold for sweet m., or in the golden variety for decorative purposes. Sow early spring in well-drained, light rich soil in sheltered position, seeds 1cm (½in) deep, thinned to 25cm (10in) apart. May also be propagated by cuttings taken in early summer, root division in spring or autumn. In very cold areas grow in pots and put in a cool greenhouse or take indoors for the winter.

Sweet m: treat as half-hardy annual in cool climates. Sow early spring in light rich soil under glass, planting out 20cm (8in) apart in early summer in a sunny sheltered spot. Ideal for growing in containers and indoors.

Wild m: easiest to grow. Sow early spring in well-drained, rich soil, preferably limed or chalky, in sheltered spot, thinned to 30cm (12in) apart. Water in dry weather. Protect roots in winter with peat or leaf mould. May also be propagated by root division in spring or autumn.

Medicinal An infusion of fresh leaves benefits the digestion and respiratory disorders, especially coughs and whooping cough. Helps to relieve headache, menstrual cramps and, used as a mouthwash and gargle, helps a sore throat. Use in a poultice for rheumatic pain and varicose veins. Use an infusion in a tonic bath for pains in the joints. NB Pot marjoram not used medicinally.

Cosmetic Use dried leaves in muslin (cheesecloth) bags to put with linen to help deter moths. Also good in potpourris.

Culinary Particularly good with meat dishes, especially game, beef, chicken, meat loaves and sausages. Also good added to tomato, marrow (summer squash), potato and stuffed vegetable dishes. Use with fish, egg and cheese dishes, and in *bouquet garni* and herb vinegars. Dried wild m. (oregano) is used sprinkled on pizzas and more sparingly than the others in all dishes.

Marshmallow (mallards, mauls, schloss tea, cheeses, mortification root, sweet weed, wymote, althea)

MALVACEAE *Althaea officinalis*

Description A hardy perennial plant up to 1.2m (4ft) high, found in damp places and coastal areas throughout Europe, western Asia, North America and Australia. Root white, sweet-tasting, sticky. Stem unbranched, woolly. Leaves downy, grey-green, serrated. Flowers light red, white or purple, five-petalled, 3-5cm (1-2in) across, clustered in leaf axils, from late summer to early autumn.

Cultivation and propagation Sow autumn, as soon as seeds are ripe, in ordinary garden soil, deeply dug and enriched with compost, in moist position. Thin to 45cm (18in) apart and protect with top-dressing of compost in winter. Keep well watered until established. May also be propagated by root division in spring or autumn.

Medicinal Use an infusion of leaves and/or flowers as a soothing gargle and as a drink for bronchial and gastric complaints. Use a decoction of the grated root (2 years old) as an eye lotion or eyewash, and for coughs, sore throats, bronchial catarrh, and for digestive and urinary problems. Good for colitis and gastric ulcers. Use grated root in a poultice or an ointment for skin irritations.

Cosmetic Use the root in an ointment for dry skin or a decoction of the root in a face pack for dry skin.

Culinary Use chopped young leaves in salads. The roots may be eaten as a vegetable, boiled and then fried in butter.

Mint

Apple mint (round-leaved mint, Egyptian mint, pineapple mint [when variegated])

LABIATAE *Mentha rotundifolia*

Description A perennial plant up to 45cm (18in) high, native to Europe, found in damp soils in ditches and waste places. Stem reddish, erect, thin, branched, hairy. Leaves green above, white and velvety beneath, oblong or round, toothed, growing directly from main stem. Flowers white to

pale mauve, on dense terminal spikes, from early to mid-autumn. Whole plant combines fragrance and taste of apples and mint. A hybrid, *M. rotundifolia* Bowles variety', is smaller with darker, woollier leaves.

Cultivation and propagation Plant rooted pieces of its long underground runners in spring or autumn. Light, moist, rich soil in sun or part shade, 5cm (2in) deep and 20cm (8in) apart. Spreads quickly so if grown in the herb bed should be kept within bounds by setting roofing slates in the soil round the plant, or growing in a bottomless container set in the ground. Suitable for container growing, if kept well watered. Keep cutting and using the fresh leaves to encourage fresh growth. The plant may need renewing every 3 or 4 years: plant outside roots from old clumps on a different site, both to preserve flavour and to guard against mint rust, a fungus disease (though apple mint is less prone to this than other mints).

Culinary Use fresh leaves in fruit salads and fruit water ices. Add to fruit cups and cold punches. Also good for making mint sauce and mint jelly.

Bergamot Mint (eau-de-cologne mint, orange mint)
LABIATAE *Mentha x piperita* var. *citrata*
Description A perennial plant up to 60cm (24in) high, native to Europe but naturalized elsewhere. Stem smooth, branched, semi-prostrate, forming leafy overground runners. Leaves dark green tinged with purple, smooth, oval or elliptical. Flowers mauve, in upper leaf axils or in rounded dense terminal spikes, from mid to late autumn. Aroma like eau-de-cologne.
Cultivation and propagation As for apple mint.
Cosmetic As for peppermint.
Culinary As for peppermint, particularly with sweet dishes. Leaves may be crystallized and used to decorate puddings.

Pennyroyal (pudding grass, English pennyroyal, run-by-the-ground, lurk-in-the ditch)
LABIATAE *Mentha pulegium*
Description A perennial plant in two forms, one prostrate, up to 15cm (6in) high, the other upright, up to 30cm (12in) high, native to Europe, North Africa and western Asia, where it is found in moist, sandy soil. Stem square, branching, taking the form of an overground runner in

prostrate types. Leaves dark green, oblong or oval, serrated, slightly hairy. Flowers mauve, in dense clusters in
leaf axils, from late summer to early autumn.

Cultivation and propagation As for apple mint. Prostrate
form makes good ground-cover. May be grown between
paving stones, on rockeries, and as a lawn. Suitable for
containers.

Medicinal Drink pennyroyal tea for coughs, bronchial
troubles, digestive disorders and menstrual pain. The fresh
leaves or an infusion make a good external application for
skin irritations, insect bites and rashes. NB Not to be used
during pregnancy or by those with kidney disease.

Cosmetic Use dried leaves in herb bags for linen and
clothes cupboards. Use an infusion of leaves as a mouthwash to sweeten breath. A pot of pennyroyal indoors and
the oil applied to the skin should repel mosquitoes and
other insects.

Culinary Add finely chopped leaves to soups and stuffings, and to new potatoes with melted butter.

Peppermint (brandy mint, lamb mint, black peppermint,
white peppermint)

LABIATAE *Mentha x piperita*

Description A perennial plant up to 60cm (24in) tall,
native to Europe and now also found wild in the eastern
USA. Stem erect, square, branched, tinged with reddish-
purple (black p.) or paler (white p.). Leaves dark green or
purplish-green, oval, deeply indented leaves. Flowers

small, mauve or white, in leaf axils and in terminal spikes from mid-summer to early autumn. Whole plant has smell of menthol.

Cultivation and propagation As for apple mint.

Medicinal Peppermint tea can be taken for insomnia, nervousness and abdominal pains, heartburn and nausea, colds, migraine and nervous headaches. The leaves may be made into a salve or bath additive for itching skin conditions. Use peppermint oil as an application for bruises, sprains and toothache. Collect leaves on a hot day, just before flowering time.

Cosmetic Use leaves in a facial steam to clear the complexion, in face packs, cleansing creams and oils, and cosmetic vinegars.

Culinary Use in soups (particularly split pea), with carrots, peas and courgettes (zucchini), and in fruit dishes, fruit drinks and in peppermint water ice.

Spearmint (garden mint, pea mint, mackerel mint, sage of Bethlehem, spire mint, lamb mint, Our Lady's mint, green mint)

LABIATAE *Mentha spicata*

Description A perennial plant up to 60cm (24in) high, native to southern Europe but naturalized in temperate climates. Stem erect, square, smooth, somewhat

branched. Leaves smooth, bright green, oblong or oval, unevenly serrated. Flowers mauve, on slender leafless spike, from late summer to early autumn.

Cultivation and propagation As for apple mint.

Medicinal As for peppermint.

Cosmetic As for peppermint. Use with other mints and bergamot in a headache cushion and in pot-pourris and to add fragrance to the bath water.

Culinary As for peppermint and also particularly good for mint sauce, mint julep, and mixed with cream cheese or yoghurt and garlic to make a spread or dip.

There are many other kinds of mint, several of them hybrids. They include curly mint *(M. crispa)*, water mint *(M. aquatica)*, horse mint *(M. sylvestris)*, ginger mint *(M. gentilis)*, and Corsican mint *(M. requienii)*, but the five described in detail are the most useful types to cultivate.

Nasturtium (Indian cress, large Indian cress, garden nasturtium)

TROPAEOLACEAE *Tropaeolum majus*

Description An annual plant between 30cm (12in) and 3m (10ft) high, native to South America but cultivated all over the world. Stem somewhat succulent, light green, branched and trailing or climbing in the tall varieties, low-growing and compact in the dwarf varieties. Leaves smooth, almost round, 5-20cm (2-8in) across, radially veined, held at right angles to stem. Flowers trumpet-shaped, spurred, red, brown, orange or yellow, 5cm (2in) wide, from early summer to first frosts. Leaves, flowers and seeds are all edible, with a peppery flavour similar to that of watercress.

Cultivation and propagation Sow late spring to early summer in ordinary to light soil in sunny position where they are to flower. Very easy to grow. Suitable for flower border, herb garden and containers. Flower best in poor soil, where they help protect neighbouring plants from pests (though not black fly, to which they are susceptible). Train climbers up trunks of trees for an effective show. Save seed from one year's plants to sow the next year.

Medicinal Use the juice or tea made from flowers, leaves or seeds (or all) for respiratory congestion and chest colds. Leaves contain iron and vitamin C. Juice or infusion may be used as an internal or external disinfectant.

Cosmetic Dried flowers add colour to pot-pourris.

Culinary Use fresh young leaves chopped in salads, in soft cheese for a dip or spread, and in sandwiches. Flowers make an attractive garnish for salads and other cold dishes. Young, green unripe seeds may be pickled and substituted for capers, or added to pickles and chutneys.

Parsley (curly parsley, Petersylinge, common parsley, garden parsley, rock parsley)

UMBELLIFERAE *Petroselinum crispum*

Description A biennial plant up to 60cm (24in) high, native to northern and central Europe but naturalized in many parts of the world. Stem erect, grooved, angular, branched. Leaves triangular, deeply incised, much curled (depending on cultivar). Flowers small, greenish-yellow or pale yellow, in flat compound umbels, from mid-summer to early autumn of second year. Seeds oval, greyish-brown, tiny.

Cultivation and propagation Sow late spring to early summer, after soil has warmed up. Rich, moist, open soil in a sheltered position in sun or partial shade. Seed can be very slow to germinate (up to 8 weeks), so is best either soaked overnight in hot water before sowing or sown in drills watered with very hot water immediately beforehand. Alternatively, seed can be sown in pots given bottom heat, and then planted out 20cm (8in) apart. Keep well watered in dry weather. For a continuous supply of fresh leaves, cover the plants with cloches in winter and make a second sowing in July or August for a spring crop. May continue for a third year if flowerheads are removed. If flowers of some of the plants are left, parsley will self-sow easily. Always pick

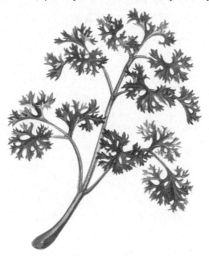

leaves from the outside of each plant, allowing new leaves to develop from the centre. Good in containers and may also be grown indoors. Can be dried but loses much flavour; freezing is a better method of preserving.

Medicinal Parsley tea made from leaves and stalks and/or seeds is good for coughs, asthma, poor digestion, rheumatism and haemorrhoids. It is also used as a tonic and diuretic, and for suppressed or difficult menstruation. Rich in vitamin C and iron.

Cosmetic Chewing the leaves sweetens the breath and removes the smell of garlic. Use an infusion as a skin lotion and to fade freckles. Use in a face pack with yoghurt or egg white for oily skin.

Culinary Parsley tends to absorb other flavours so is best used in bland dishes in generous quantities. Use chopped leaves and stems (which have more flavour) in salads, soups, sauces, mayonnaise, egg dishes, as an ingredient in *bouquet garni*, and to make parsley soup. Use sprigs fried as an accompaniment to fish, and fresh as a garnish.

Purslane (green purslane, portulaca)

PORTULACACEAE *Portulaca oleracea*

Description A half-hardy annual plant up to 15cm (6in) high, native to southern Europe, India and Asia but naturalized in central Europe. Stem thick, round, smooth, red-

dish, succulent, brittle. Leaves fleshy, oval, green, 1-2cm (½-1in) long, growing directly from main stem. Flowers small, yellow, five-petalled, growing singly or in groups of two or three from leaf axils and at the top of the plant, in late summer. Leaves and seeds have a fresh, spicy, slightly salty taste.

Cultivation and propagation Sow successively from late spring after danger of frost has passed, to mid-summer in light, well-drained, preferably sandy soil in sun. Thin seedlings to 10cm (4in) apart. Keep well watered in dry weather. Grows fast and is ready to pick after about 6 weeks when the shoots are about 7cm (3in) long. Harvest before flowering, or the leaves will be too tough to use. Can be container grown.

Medicinal Drink an infusion of the leaves and/or seeds as a tonic and laxative, and to stimulate the appetite. High vitamin C content. Diuretic.

Culinary Use young leaves in salads, soups and soft cheese for a dip. Also good in egg dishes and with cooked vegetables. Add in last few minutes of cooking time. Boil whole leaves and young shoots as a vegetable with a buttery sauce. Stems cut into sections may be pickled.

Rose (dog briar [for dog rose]; eglantine [for sweetbriar])
ROSACEAE *Rosa canina* (dog rose), *R. eglanteria* (sweet-briar)

Description All are erect or climbing perennial shrubs up to 3m (10ft) high, native to Europe, North Africa and western Asia. Stem thorny, hooked in *R. canina*. Leaves oval, pointed, serrated, smooth, up to 4cm (2in) long. Flowers large, aromatic, particularly in *R. eglanteria,* white or pink, usually single and five-petalled, in mid to late summer. Fruit (hip) fleshy, rounded, red or orange, shiny, in autumn.

Cultivation and propagation Found wild, and usually cultivated as hybrids. Plant cuttings or rooted plants in early spring or late autumn. Rich, well-drained soil in sun, 1m (3¼ft) apart. Strong-growing so make sure there is plenty of space. Good against a fence or trellis at the back of a border, and as a hedge. Gather rose petals in summer when they are just coming into flower and the scent is strongest. Leave hips on plant until after first frost, when they should be picked and used at once, or dried or pureed.

Medicinal Drink an infusion of dried petals for headache and dizziness. An infusion of the hips acts as a tonic and mild diuretic, and helps to relieve colds. Use a strong infusion of the hips in a poultice to relieve puffiness round the eyes.

Cosmetic Rose lotion, made from dried petals and white wine vinegar (2 tablespoons to 2 cups, left for 3 weeks and strained) added to rosewater (1 cup), makes a good astringent for oily skin. Dried petals for pot-pourris and herb cushions.

Culinary Petals can be used in wine and fruit cups, in jams and, when candied or crystallized, for cake decoration. Use rose hip puree to make wine and a cordial, as a sauce or jelly for game and cold meats, puddings and ice cream.

Rosemary (dew of the sea, polar plant, compass weed, herb of remembrance)

LABIATAE *Rosmarinus officinalis*

Description An evergreen perennial shrub up to 2m (6ft) high, but more commonly 1.2m (4ft), native to the Mediterranean region but widely cultivated since earliest times. Stem downy when young, becoming woody with scaly, ash-coloured bark, branched. Leaves narrow, leathery, up to 3cm (1½in) long, with a prominent vein down the centre, smooth and dark green above, downy and white underneath. Flowers pale blue, sometimes white, small, growing in clusters in leaf axils from late spring to early summer. Whole plant aromatic.

Cultivation and propagation Sow spring, but very slow to grow from seed. Best grown from 15-20cm (6-9in) long cuttings of non-flowering shoots, preferably with a heel, taken in late summer and put in water where they should form roots. Plant out and give cloche protection during first winter in poor, well-drained, light sandy soil, preferably chalky or limed, in sunny sheltered spot. Slow growing. Can be container grown, particularly a dwarf variety. Can also be propagated by root division in late autumn or early spring. May be gathered fresh all year round.

Medicinal An infusion of leaves improves the digestion and circulation, and relieves headaches. A salve made from the oil may be used externally for bruises, sores, eczema, rheumatism, neuralgia, and as an insect repellent. Fresh leaves may be applied to stings and bites.

Cosmetic Use an infusion as a hair rinse for dark hair. Use in a muslin (cheesecloth) bag for a tonic bath. Use leaves for a refreshing foot bath, in a cleansing cream for normal to dry skin, in an infusion for a skin freshening lotion and for a mouthwash to sweeten the breath.

Culinary Traditional use with roast lamb but may also be used with chicken, duck and fish. Use in stuffings and marinades, egg and cheese dishes, and in biscuits (cookies),scones, jams, jellies and wine and fruit cups as a garnish. Unless young leaves are used, chopped very small, best to remove fresh leaves or sprigs before serving as they are tough and spiky. Dried leaves crumble easily.

Sage (garden sage)

LABIATAE *Salvia officinalis*

Description An evergreen perennial shrub 30-45cm (12-18in) high, native to southern Europe, especially the Mediterranean, where it is found in limestone soils on sunny slopes. Stem square, downy, woody at the base. Leaves oblong, rough-textured, pitted, dusty-looking, usually pale grey-green but some forms have variegated or purple-tinged leaves. Flowers violet-blue to pale purple, two lipped, on terminal spikes in mid-summer.

Cultivation and propagation Sow early spring under glass for transplanting into open ground in early summer. Alternatively, take 15cm (6in) cuttings with a heel in late spring and plant in open ground. Light, well-drained soil in sun, 40-45cm (16-18in) apart. Old leggy plants should be earthed up in spring and layered. Cut off rooted cuttings in autumn and plant out. Not a long-lived plant, so should be replaced every 4 years or so. May also be propagated by root division in spring. To harvest for drying, gather sprigs just

before flowering and hang upside down protected from dust by paper.

Medicinal Sage tea reduces perspiration. Also useful if taken for a few days by lactating mothers after weaning, to help stop the flow of milk. Tea also good for respiratory tract infection, nervous conditions such as anxiety and depression, and as a gargle for sore throats, tonsilitis and laryngitis. Crushed fresh leaves may be applied to insect bites.

Cosmetic Use the leaves in a facial steam to cleanse and refine skin. An infusion of the leaves makes a good mouthwash, hair conditioner and astringent cleansing lotion. Use crushed leaves with pureed apple as a face pack for normal skin and a strong infusion with milk and alum as a face pack for oily skin.

Culinary Use finely chopped leaves sparingly in sage and onion stuffing for roast pork and with other meat dishes, in onion soups and sauces, cooked tomato dishes, and in cream cheese dips. Add with other herbs to omelettes, cheese dishes, bread and scones.

Salad burnet (burnet, garden burnet)

ROSACEAE *Poterium sanguisorba*

Description A perennial plant 30-60cm (12-24in) high, native to dry, chalky soils of the Mediterranean region but naturalized in other parts of Europe and North America. Stems slender, grooved, branching. Leaves oblong, coarsely serrated, in pairs. Flowers small, greenish with purple-red stamens, in a dense rounded head at the end of a stem growing from the centre of the plant, in early to mid-summer.

Cultivation and propagation Sow spring or autumn in good well-drained garden soil, in sun or partial shade. Will seed itself, though for use as a herb do not allow to flower, and keep cut back to encourage production of new leaves, which have a cucumber-like flavour. (Old leaves are bitter.) May be cut for use all year round; always use fresh. May be propagated by division of roots in spring or autumn, but it is better to sow new seed every year for a supply of young leaves. Suitable for containers and as an edging plant.

Medicinal Drink a tea made from the leaves as a tonic, to reduce fever, to stimulate kidney function, and for haemorrhoids and diarrhoea. Chewing the fresh leaves aids

digestion. A decoction of the root may be applied to cuts to stop bleeding.

Cosmetic Use an infusion of the leaves as a lotion to cleanse and refine the skin, in a face pack and facial steam. Leaves in a muslin (cheesecloth) bag added to the water make a refreshing bath.

Culinary Mainly used as a salad herb as its name suggests; also good as a garnish for cold dishes and drinks, and in soups and sauces where a cucumber flavour is required. Use in burnet vinegar and add chopped leaves to soft cheese for a dip or spread.

Savory (bean herb [for summer savory]; mountain savory [for winter savory])

LABIATAE *Satureja hortensis* (summer savory), *Satureja montana* (winter savory)

Description Summer savory is an annual plant up to 45cm (18in) high, native to the eastern Mediterranean region and southwest Asia, but naturalized in many warm parts of the world. Stem erect, bushy, hairy, often becoming purplish with age, branching. Leaves small, long, narrow, sometimes with hairy margins. Flowers small, two-lipped, pink, pale mauve or white, in sparse clusters, from mid-summer to early autumn. Whole plant aromatic, with a pungent, spicy flavour not unlike that of marjoram.

Winter savory is a perennial plant up to 30cm (12in) high, native to southeast Europe and North Africa. Similar in appearance to summer savory but more woody and bristly and less delicate in flavour, with flowers in terminal spikes.

Cultivation and propagation Sow early spring under glass or late spring in open ground in light, rich soil in sun (summer s.); poor, dry, chalky soil in sun (winter s.). Thin to 15cm (6in) apart. Winter s. may also be propagated by root division in spring or autumn, by cuttings in early summer, or by layering. Winter s. takes a year to grow from seed to a good-sized plant; summer s. is ready to use from early summer, and if plants are cut to 2cm (1in) from the base they will produce a second crop of leaves. Both may be container grown.

Medicinal Drink an infusion of the leaves to aid digestion and stimulate the appetite, and as a gargle for a sore throat. Rub the fresh leaves on bee and wasp stings to relieve the pain.

Culinary Use in meat, fish and egg dishes, in stuffings and all bean dishes. Use chopped and sprinkled on soups, in sauces and vegetable dishes. Add a sprig to wine vinegar and leave to permeate.

Southernwood (old man, lad's love, artemisia)
COMPOSITAE *Artemisia abrotanum*
Description A perennial plant up to 1m (3¼ft) high,
native to southern Europe and naturalized in North America. Stem woody, bushy. Leaves feathery, finely divided,
somewhat downy, grey-green, 7cm (3in) long, smelling
strongly of lemon. Flowers very small, inconspicuous, pale
yellow, in late summer to early autumn (but rarely flowering
in temperate climates).

Cultivation and propagation Grow from young green cuttings 15cm (6in) long taken in summer, or from heeled
cuttings from old wood in autumn. Set 7cm (3in) deep in
sand until rooted. Good, well-drained soil in a sunny,
sheltered spot. Cut back established plants in mid-spring
to keep them bushy and compact. May also be propagated
by root division in autumn and by layering.
Medicinal Use the tea as a tonic to aid digestion and
relieve catarrh.
Cosmetic Use an infusion of leaves as a hair rinse and to
scent bath water. Use dried leaves in a muslin (cheesecloth) bag to scent cupboards and drawers, and to repel
moths. Stems make a yellow dye. The attractive foliage can
be used in floral decorations.

Culinary Add chopped leaves and other herbs to salads, and use in sweet dishes.

Sweet Cicely (British myrrh, European sweet Cicely, anise, great chervil, giant sweet chervil, smooth Cicely, shepherd's needle, sweet fern)

UMBELLIFERAE *Myrrhis odorata*

Description A perennial plant up to 90cm (36in) high, native to Europe where it is found in meadows, heaths and hedgerows. Stem grooved, hollow, branching. Leaves

large, soft, lacy, downy, bright green above and paler beneath. Flowers small, white, in umbels, from early to mid-spring. Fruit long, ridged, black, 2cm (1in) long. Whole plant edible, with sweet anise flavour.

Cultivation and propagation Sow early spring in good moist soil in partial shade, where the plants are to grow. Thin to 45cm (18in) apart; transplants easily. Slow growing but plants self-sow readily once established. May also be propagated by root division in early spring: cut the taproots into sections, each with a bud, and plant 5cm (2in) deep.

Medicinal Make a tea from the leaves or chew the ripe seeds for indigestion. May be used as a sugar substitute for diabetics.

Culinary Use chopped fresh leaves and chopped green seeds in salads. Use leaves with tart fruits and in jam making to reduce acidity and save on sugar. Use leaves to garnish sweet and savoury dishes, in cakes, cold drinks, and boiled as a vegetable. Add leaves or seeds to the water when cooking cabbage. Add the boiled, cold root to salads.

Tarragon (little dragon, estragon [for French tarragon]; false tarragon [for Russian tarragon])

COMPOSITAE *Artemisia dracunculus* (French tarragon) *Artemisia dracunculoides* (Russian tarragon)

Description A perennial shrub up to 1m (3¼ft) high (or taller in Russian variety), native to southern and central Asia, but naturalized in warm parts of the USA and Europe.

Stem erect, branched, smooth. Leaves narrow, about 5cm (2in) long, smooth, with unserrated margins. Flowers small, whitish-green or pale yellow, woolly, drooping, almost globular, from mid- to late summer (though they do not open properly in a temperate climate). Whole plant aromatic; Russian tarragon is greatly inferior in flavour, and not as good for culinary use.

Cultivation and propagation Does not set seed in temperate climates. Grow from rooted cuttings taken in spring or from pieces of root taken in spring or autumn. Good, well-drained soil in sunny, sheltered position, 30cm (12in) apart. Needs feeding during growing season to reach its full flavour. Russian t. is winter-hardy, but French t. may need winter protection, especially when young, by mulching with compost or straw. Every 4 years plants should be divided and replanted in fresh soil in early spring. May be container grown. Harvest in July for preserving; better frozen than dried.

Medicinal Drink an infusion of the leaves to promote digestion and stimulate the appetite, and to help overcome insomnia. Make a herb pillow of tarragon with other herbs to aid sleep.

Culinary Use fresh sprigs to make tarragon vinegar. Use fresh leaves to garnish cold savoury dishes, in light soups and sauces, in mayonnaise for fish, in herb butter and French dressing. Good with chicken, fish, eggs, and in mild-flavoured vegetable dishes and salads.

Thyme (garden thyme, English thyme, French thyme [for common thyme])

LABIATAE *Thymus vulgaris* (common thyme), *Thymus x citriodorus* (lemon thyme)

Description A perennial evergreen shrub 20-30cm (8-12in) high, native to the Mediterranean region and

cultivated worldwide. Stem quadrangular, woody, some-what prostrate and gnarled. Leaves very small, slightly downy, oval to elliptic, grey-green in common t.; variable from dark to light or variegated in lemon t. Flowers small, pale mauve to deep pink, in dense or loosely clustered terminal heads, from mid- to late summer, or later in common t. Both plants aromatic, lemon t. with a strong lemon scent. There are gold- and silver-variegated varieties of lemon t., and lemon-scented varieties of common t.

Cultivation and propagation Sow early summer in light, well-drained soil in sunny, sheltered spot. Space lemon t. plants 30cm (12in) apart; common t. plants 45cm (18in) apart. Lemon t. is less hardy than common t. so winter protection may be necessary in cold climates; mulch sur-rounding soil with straw or leaf mould. Replace every 3 years when centres begin to die, by cuttings taken in spring to autumn or root division in spring. May also be layered from mid-spring to early summer: earth up the plant so that only the green tips protrude, and roots will form on the stems in the soil, for planting out in mid- to late summer. Both types good for rockeries, between paving stones, and in containers. Harvest for drying when they begin to flower (take non-flowering shoots). Better to use dried thyme in winter than fresh, which loses its flavour then; thyme retains its pungency well when dried.

Medicinal Common t: use a tincture, extract or infusion for throat and bronchial infections, coughs, diarrhoea and lack of appetite. A hot infusion relieves flatulence and indigestion and helps promote sleep. Oil of thyme (thymol) has an antiseptic action for which it is used in mouth-washes and toothpastes, and to treat intestinal worms. Use a salve or oil to treat shingles, spots and pimples.

Cosmetic Common t: use an infusion of flowers and leaves as a skin tonic, and in a soothing facial steam. The oil is widely used in cosmetic preparations.
Lemon t: add leaves in a muslin (cheesecloth) bag to the bath water. Dried leaves and flowers can be used in herb cushions and pot-pourris.

Culinary Use leaves as an ingredient in *bouquet garni* for many soups, sauces, and stock, particularly tomato soup. May be used in all savoury dishes, especially egg and fish dishes, meat, poultry and game, stuffings and cheese dishes. Lemon t. is particularly good in a stuffing for chicken, with fish, and sprinkled over cooked vegetables and in fruit salads, jellies and baked custard.

Wild thyme *(Thymus serpyllum)* exists in many forms but is particularly suitable as an aromatic carpeting herb in the garden.

Valerian (garden heliotrope, phu, phew, all-heal, setwall, cat's valerian, fragrant valerian, common valerian, English valerian, German valerian, wild valerian, vandal root)

VALERIANACEAE *Valeriana officinalis*

Description A perennial plant up to about 1m (3¼ft) high, native to Europe and western Asia, naturalized in North America. Root is a short rhizome with straggly roots, yellow-brown, fragrant. Stem hollow, angular, furrowed. Leaves large, deeply divided into sharply serrated leaflets. Flowers small, pink or white, fragrant, in terminal clusters in mid-summer.

Cultivation and propagation Sow in spring under glass; slow to germinate. Damp, well-drained soil in sun. Plant

out seedlings in summer about 60cm (24in) apart. Remove flowering stems in summer to encourage rootstock (only part used) to enlarge. Harvest rhizomes at the end of the second season, in autumn, after leaves have died down. Remove fibrous roots before using or drying, but take care not to cut or bruise the rhizome when first lifted as it will emit an unpleasant, rancid smell. May also be propagated by root division in spring or autumn.

Medicinal Drink a decoction or infusion of the root for nervous tension and exhaustion, anxiety, headaches, migraine, insomnia, intestinal cramps, and with other remedies for high blood-pressure. Take an infusion internally and as a wash externally for sores and pimples.

Culinary The root, in small quantities, can be used as a flavour in cooking, though its use has largely died out.

Watercress (scurvy grass, tall nasturtium)

CRUCIFERAE *Nasturtium officinale*

Description An aquatic perennial plant from 30-60cm (12-24in) high, native to Europe but naturalized in the USA and elsewhere. Found in streams and ditches. Stem hollow, branching, creeping through water then growing upright above the surface. Leaves dark green, smooth, somewhat fleshy, oblong to roundish. Flowers small, white, in terminal clusters, from early summer to mid-autumn. Edible leaves and stems have strong, peppery flavour.

Cultivation and propagation Sow summer or autumn, in boxes. Plant out seedlings 15cm (6in) apart in rich sandy soil in clean running water in an open position. Soil should be 7cm (3in) deep and the water 10cm (4in) deep. May be grown in rich, moist garden soil if watered frequently, but will taste more pungent. May also be propagated by cuttings taken in spring or early autumn and rooted in water. Cut constantly to produce bushy plants and to prevent them flowering. Always use fresh.

Medicinal High vitamin C and iron content make it a good illness preventative. Drink an infusion of young shoots for rheumatic pains, digestive upsets and bronchial catarrh and coughs. NB Not to be taken by those with kidney problems or during pregnancy.

Cosmetic Use the juice of leaves and stems as an application for skin blemishes.

Culinary Use in salads and as a garnish, and to make watercress soup, delicious hot or cold. Use chopped leaves instead of mustard and pepper in cream sauce (especially good with fish) and as a filling for omelettes.

Woodruff (sweet woodruff, wuderove, woodrova, waldmeister tea, master of the wood, woodward)

RUBIACEAE *Asperula odorata*

Description A perennial plant up to 15-20cm (6-8in) high, found in woods and gardens in Europe, Asia and

North Africa; introduced to USA. Rootstock thin, creeping, with numerous, matted roots. Stem slender, square, smooth, shiny. Leaves in whorls of 6, dark green, narrow, pointed, soft but with rough edges. Flowers small, white, bell- or funnel-shaped, four-petalled, in loose branching clusters in early summer. Whole plant smells of new-mown hay, becoming stronger when the herb is cut and dried.

Cultivation and propagation Sow late summer. Slow to germinate. Ordinary soil in shade. Thin to 20cm (8in) apart. Spreads quite quickly by root runners. May also be propagated by root division of established plants after flowering. Makes a good ground-cover plant under trees and shrubs, and in shady borders.

Medicinal Drink woodruff tea made from the dried leaves and flowers for stomach pain, especially when it is associated with obstructions such as gall stones. Tea also good for the liver, and helps relieve insomnia, migraine and neuralgia, and nervous conditions.

Cosmetic Use dried leaves and flowers in pot-pourris, herb sachets and pillows, and for scenting linen (or any other items which are stored in cupboards) to remove mustiness and repel moths.

Culinary Add partially dried whole leaves and stems to apple juice and wine cups for a delicious flavour. Flowers and leaves make a delicious tea.

Yarrow (milfoil, carpenter's weed, woundwort, nosebleed, old man's pepper, staunchweed, devil's nettle, toothache weed, noble yarrow, sanguinary, thousandleaf)

COMPOSITAE *Achillea millefolium*

Description A hardy perennial up to 60cm (24in) high, native to Europe but widely found in fields, waste places and along roadsides in temperate regions. Stem round, smooth, grooved, branched near the top. Leaves dark green, slightly hairy, oval in outline and divided into many feathery segments. Flowers white or pinkish, small, growing in flat-topped clusters from early summer to autumn. Leaves (which have a strong, slightly bitter flavour) and flowers may both be used.

Cultivation and propagation Plant spring or autumn, from rooted plant taken from the wild. Any soil in sun or partial shade. Easy to grow and needs little attention. May be propagated by root division, but spreads easily and may need to have the roots cut back from time to time to keep the plant within bounds. Helps neighbouring plants to resist disease and seems to deepen the fragrance and flavour of nearby herbs.

Medicinal Drink yarrow tea for lack of appetite, indigestion, flatulence and other problems of the digestive tract. Also good for liver problems, internal bleeding (such as nosebleeds, rectal bleeding, excessive menstrual flow), and as a general tonic for the blood. Use a decoction as a wash for all kinds of wounds and sores, and for chapped skin. An application of the fresh leaf alleviates toothache. Combine with elderflowers and peppermint in an infusion for colds and influenza. NB Extended use may make the skin sensitive to light.

Cosmetic Use an infusion of the fresh flowers as a lotion or in a face pack or facial steam for greasy skin; add to the bath water for a relaxing bath. A decoction or infusion of the leaves may be applied to the scalp to stimulate hair growth and to stop hair falling out.

Culinary Use chopped leaves in salads and mixed with soft cheese for a spread or dip. Substitute for hops in brewing.

Plant index

General index

PDO 81-238